MASKS OF CHAROS
IN MODERN GREEK DEMOTIC SONGS

MICHAŁ BZINKOWSKI

MASKS OF CHAROS
IN MODERN GREEK DEMOTIC SONGS
SOURCES, REPRESENTATIONS AND CONTEXT

Jagiellonian University Press

Reviewer
dr hab. Dariusz Brodka, prof. UJ

Cover design
Paweł Sepielak

With the financial support of the Institute of Classical Philology of the Faculty of Philology at the Jagiellonian University

ISBN 978-83-233-4330-1
ISBN 978-83-233-9698-7 (e-book)

JAGIELLONIAN UNIVERSITY PRESS

www.wuj.pl

Jagiellonian University Press
Editorial Offices: Michałowskiego 9/2, 31-126 Kraków
Phone: +48 12 663 23 80, +48 12 663 23 82, Fax: +48 12 663 23 83
Distribution: Phone: +48 12 631 01 97, Fax: +48 12 631 01 98
Cell Phone: +48 506 006 674, e-mail: sprzedaz@wuj.pl
Bank: PEKAO SA, IBAN PL80 1240 4722 1111 0000 4856 3325

Αγγελικό και μαύρο, φως
Γιώργος Σεφέρης
Light, angelic and black
George Seferis

In Memory of my Grandparents

CONTENTS

PREFACE

Charon or Charos?

On 21st August 1912, the *Montreal Daily Star* published an interesting statement entitled significantly: "NO CHARON HERE. He is All Very Good for the World Beneath." The Royal Netherlands Steamship Company was forced to change the name of its ship because of Greek dockers, who had unexpectedly boycotted the steamship that moored in a Greek port. The note in the newspaper said that "the men refused to work the ship on account of its association with the mythological old gentleman, who plies the ferry across the river of the lower world."[1]

Both the incident and the explanation are quite meaningful. Firstly, they show a complete misunderstanding of the West Europeans of the reaction of Greek workers. The mythological person they were so afraid of was obviously not the Ancient Greek Charon, but the modern figure of Charos – personified Death – that retained his name (and perhaps some features, which I shall discuss later), and is deeply rooted in folk culture as well as in the Modern Greek conscience. Secondly, such a sudden and resolute reaction of the dockers may confirm the vitality of Charos in Greek culture and the negative connotation that his name evokes among Greeks.

The ancient ferryman of the dead, whose name was inherited by Charos (Χάρος), the modern personification of death, was rather neglected in the pantheon of Greek gods and appears very rarely in Ancient Greek literature.[2] His name as well as his person are most probably

---

[1] I cite the whole passage from Rose 1913: 247.

[2] I have already outlined the question in my paper Bzinkowski 2009: 17–22. Charon occurs, among others, in the epic poem "Minyas" cited by Pausanias (10.18.1),

of Semitic origin[3] and the concept of a boatman or a ferryman on the rivers of death was known in the ancient Near East.[4]

In the European conscience, Charon is mostly associated with his representation in Dante's *Inferno*, where he appears as an old man with fiery eyes and is demonic in appearance (Canto III, 82–128). Dante, in turn, did not create such a picture but borrowed it from Virgil's *Aeneid* (VI, 299–301), where Charon appears to be even more odious. These two images of the ferryman of the dead influenced all the later writers and painters in European tradition who in any way alluded to him.[5]

The Modern Greek Charos, at least the way he is depicted in demotic songs, as we shall see, has nothing in common with the ancient and medieval representations of Charon. He is not an ugly looking old man, white-haired, white-bearded and dressed in rags, nor a ferryman carrying the souls to the Underworld across the river. However, for the West Europeans who see his name in the modern Hellenic version, he brings to mind only unequivocal associations.

Such a stereotypical view may partly originate in the seeming similarity of one of the well-known representations of the Modern Greek Charos, according to which he leads the dead, which I shall present in subsequent parts of the present book,[6] but mostly is a result of the ignorance of contemporary Greek culture – a phenomenon typical for the rest of Europeans, at least from the nineteenth century, when Europe started to recover the cradle of its civilization together with the Philhellenic movement, and after the Greek War of Independence 1821–1833. It would not be an oversimplification to say that the burden of the classical past still lies heavily on the perception of Modern Greece.

---

in Aristophanes (*Ranae* 182), in the "Dialogues with the dead" of Lucian of Samosat (*Charon* 8, Loeb ed. 2.412), and in Diodor of Sicily (1.92.96). On black-figured pottery Charon appears no earlier than c. 500 BC and in the second quarter of the fifth century we find him on white-ground *lekythoi*. Sourvinou-Inwood 1995: 301 f.

[3] Blažek 2007: 155 ff.

[4] In the Gilgamesh epic, we come across the ferryman Urshanabi (or Arad-Ea). Babylonians and Assyrians also knew Hamar-tabal (or Humuttabal). In Egyptian mythology the role of someone leading the dead to the Underworld was played by Anubis. Terpening 1985: 13 f. Prioreschi 1990: 124 f. The Etruscan Charun is said to have been introduced to Etruria by the Greeks. Terpening 1985: 14.

[5] Terpening 1985: 11 f.

[6] See the chapter "Charos *nekropompos*."

Similarly, as Modern Greece is not just a continuation of the Ancient one, the modern Charos is in no case a simple counterpart of the ancient Charon, nor an elaboration of the idea of the ferryman of the dead. He is definitely someone else and I shall attempt to elucidate who he is exactly in the present book.

* * *

The figure of Charos (Χάρος) is widespread in the whole Hellenic world, including Cyprus and the Pontus region, where he is called Charondas (Χάροντας).[7] Yet, in spite of the fact that his name is well-known for every Greek, it would not be an exaggeration if I said that even for them – due to the variety and complexity of his representations – he constitutes an intangible personality around whom many common stereotypes have inevitably arisen. Thus, any simple answers given for the question of who Charos is – for instance: he is death or a personification of death,[8] a black rider on a black horse, a reaper with a scythe etc. – are only partly true, because the question is far more complicated.

The question of Charos obviously has already been the subject of research, during which many attempts have been made to approach his personality with different results and using quite different methodology. Some of them, although they still bring a lot of extremely interesting data and are well-documented, are a little outdated (Schmidt 1871; Hesseling 1897, 1931; Waser 1898; Moravcsik 1931). The other ones, so far the most valuable, focus only on some particular aspects of the figure of Charos, paying attention to possible historical connotations (Saunier 1972, 1982, 1993). There are also some more general papers outlining this mythological figure in demotic songs, such as the paper by Alexiou (1978) or an article which is full of interesting examples by Omatos (1990). On Greek ground still the most comprehensive study, although not concentrated fully on Charos, but generally on the eschatology of Modern

---

[7] As far as I know, the only exception is the Greek diaspora in South Italy, where we come across exclusively the notion *tánato*.

[8] Gr. *thanatos* (θάνατος) as a common noun for death is not personified in Modern Greek culture.

Greek folk songs, is the unpublished doctoral dissertation by Anagnostopoulos (1984).

As a matter of fact, the present book is the first one that aims to explore different representations of Charos in demotic songs and to outline, where it is feasible to some extent, the possible sources of their origin, as well as to sketch the broader context in which they occur. The investigation into the indefinable personality of Charos is beset by countless difficulties that I will touch upon in the course of this book.

Chapter I deals with the sources of the demotic songs in which the figure of Charos appears, within the framework of growing interest in the nineteenth century of European intellectuals in the folk culture that somehow accompanied the romantic movement. Furthermore, I also briefly present the category of *mirologia* songs (dirges) and their relation to the *songs of the Underworld and Charos.*

Chapter II explores the representations: firstly of the Modern Greek Underworld, the domain of Charos, and secondly of different images of Charos. The main criteria used here in the selection of examples are based: on one hand, on concise, as if only suggested, representations of Charos mainly tangible through some fixed phrases and epithets, and, on the other, on Charos' activities influencing human actions, in other words, the representations in which he appears to be an "active" personage.

Finally, in chapter III I present the most elaborated representations of Charos that demand to be shown in a broader context connected with their supposed origins, as well as the possible influences of other, literary and cultural, traditions. In this chapter I also deal with relations of the figure of Charos with other persons.

This book is not meant to be a holistic approach to the phenomenon of Charos in Modern Greek culture. I realize that both the selected examples from demotic songs and the chosen method of research, mainly philologically orientated, also including in some cases a comparative as well as linguistic approach, only partly shed some light on the complexity of the question. The research I have attempted to conduct, trying to display as fully as possible the variety of the representations of Charos in demotic songs, required references to different historical levels of Greek history, including Ancient Greece and Byzantium. It was also indispensable, here and there, to allude to some ethnographical accounts and especially to different literary texts in which the figure of Charos appears, mainly from Crete and the islands for centuries under West European influence. The folk tradition, to which undoubtedly the written demotic songs belong, also encompasses the coexistence of the earlier, archaic elements of pre-Christian tradition mingled with Christian ones belonging to the Orthodox Church and inherited from Byzantium. All of this makes every attempt at carrying out a holistic approach to the question of Charos extremely difficult and demands a lot of intertextual and intercultural interferences. Yet, I do hope my study will be useful for all those who research the relations between Ancient, Byzantine and Modern Greek culture, who deal with the folk tradition of Greece and of the Balkans, as well as for those who are interested in the history of ideas. Hopefully, it will constitute an enticement to further explore the eschatology of Modern Greek folk songs that, in my opinion, deserves special attention as it goes back to the most archaic concepts of the afterlife beliefs and, thus, to the most archetypal human thinking.

* * *

Lastly, let me make two final remarks. Due to the fact that I have dealt with the question of Charos and the eschatology of Modern Greek demotic songs over the years, the present book contains some fragments of my previous papers, which I always try to highlight. Two of them have been incorporated almost wholly,[9] while I have used only fragments of the other ones, which I had the opportunity to deliver at some international conferences, while presenting the results of my research.[10]

Secondly, writing this book would not be possible without the support of some libraries, where I had the pleasure and opportunity to work. I am very grateful especially to the Library of Medieval and Modern Greek Studies and the Library of Folklore and Social Anthropology at the Aristotle University of Thessaloniki, the Library of Institut für

[9] Bzinkowski 2011b; 2015a.

[10] These are my talks about Charos in demotic songs I delivered in the 4th and 5th European Congresses of Modern Greek Studies (Granada 2010, Thessaloniki 2014), and International Conference on Modern Greek Language, Literature, History and Civilization (Poznań 2015).

Byzantinistik und Neogräzistik at the University of Vienna, Biblioteca Interdipartimentale "Tito Livio" of the University of Padova, the Institute of Classical Studies Library at the University of London, the Warburg Institute Library in London, the Library of the Institute of Classical Studies in Skopje, and the Library of Hellenic Studies at the University of Warsaw.

Finally, I extend my heartfelt gratitude to all my colleagues and friends who helped and encouraged me constantly during my work.

Special thanks to my nearest and dearest angel who constantly helped me during the final months of the writing process, giving me strength and warm support and patiently listening to and discussing crucial and complicated issues of Greek folk songs.

Chapter I

SOURCES

1. Folk songs in nineteenth- and twentieth-century Greece

Although the beginning of studies on folklore is considered to be the second half of the nineteenth century, when J.G Herder published his famous work,[11] the process of creating modern states by independent nations in nineteenth-century Europe brought about an increasing interest in seeking national roots in folk tradition.[12] The term "folklore" as a national feature, although still obscure as a notion at that time, became in the course of the century the subject of studies on national culture.[13]

Paradoxically, except for Germany, where the interest in folklore studies had undoubtedly begun, in other West European countries with strong national identity, such as France and Great Britain, the process had to wait several decades.[14] Yet in those areas that, due to historical causation, were characterized by the lack of continuity of national distinctiveness, the value of folklore studies was more meaningful and contributed to a great extent to the crystallization of national identity.

---

[11] *Alte Volkslieder*, 1775, soon published in a two-volume edition (1778–1779). Politis A. 2011: 234. Interestingly, at the end of the eighteenth and beginning of the nineteenth century, when the folk culture started to be discovered, it already began vanishing. Burke 1978: 3.

[12] Politis A. 2011: 235–236.

[13] A comprehensive survey of the beginning of growing interest in folklore in eighteenth- and nineteenth-century Europe is given by Burke 1978: 3–22.

[14] The first publication of French demotic songs is 1840 (Tieghem 1948: 301–311). Politis A. 2011: 234.

The national renaissance of the Slavonic nations separating from the great nineteenth-century empires is the best example of the above-mentioned tendency.[15] In this respect, the folklore of Balkan Slavs deserves special attention. It has already been thoroughly researched, with Vuk Stefanović Karadžić's two volumes of Serbian Folk Songs (Српске народне пјесме), published in 1814 and 1815, resulting in enormous international success, enchanting intellectuals, writers and researchers all over Europe.[16] Their influence on famous European writers belonging to the romantic movement is well-known and has been the subject of many detailed studies.[17] Their transnational circulation influenced the most famous writers of that epoch, such as the Brothers Grimm, Goethe, Pushkin and the greatest Polish romantic poet Adam Mickiewicz, professor of Slavic Literature at the Collège de France.[18] Of course, the question of the attitude of popular culture to the so-called high culture and their mutual relationship is a separate complicated subject of studies. What is yet worth underlining is that no earlier than in romanticism was folklore evoked to an unprecedented depth that is a form of its imitation.[19]

The interest of West Europeans towards Greece came some time later, together with the outbreak of the War of Independence in 1821, when Europe reminded itself about the descendants of Ancient Greeks and their culture. The Philhellenic movement was followed by Charles Claude Fauriel's well-known collection of Modern Greek folk songs in a bilingual French-Greek edition, including the collector's comprehen-

---

[15] Burke 1978: 12–13.

[16] The work of Karadžić was firstly known and admired in Europe thanks to a famous Slovene linguist and philologist working in Vienna, Jernej Bartol Kopitar (1780–1844), who translated the collection into German and shared it with Jakob Grimm and Goethe in 1814. See Ibrovac 1966: 272 and especially the chapter: "The network between Jernej Kopitar and Vuk Karadžić" in Merchiers' biography of Kopitar: Merchier 2007: 222–287. For more on intellectuals' interest in folk culture, see Burke 1978: 8–9. On Karadžić see also Burke 1978: 13.

[17] Both Goethe and Herder, who gave them European fame, had known Serbian songs long before Karadžić's collection. See Ibrovac 1966: 260.

[18] For a detailed reception of Karadžić's collection, see Ibrovac 1966: 270–285.

[19] Wrocławski 2011: 21.

sive introduction[20] and commentary on the folk tradition and particular songs.[21]

It is yet uncertain if Fauriel, who was to introduce Modern Greek folk songs to Europe ten years later, had known the above-mentioned Karadžić's collection and their author before 1826, due to the fact that the work of the Serbian linguist was veiled in France by a conspiracy of silence up to 1819.[22] Undoubtedly, he must have had the French translation of the collection, published in two volumes in Leipzig in 1823–1825 (*Chants populaires serbes*). Nevertheless, his lecture at the Collège de France that he gave in the years 1831–1832 was devoted both to Serbian and Modern Greek folk songs.[23]

Fauriel's *Chants populaires de la Grèce moderne*, edited in Paris in 1824–1825, became unquestionably one of the most popular collections of folk songs at that time and its influence was really impressive.[24] It was indeed the very first publication of Modern Greek folk songs in Europe as a separate collection, although some attempts had been unsuccessfully made before Fauriel.[25]

---

[20] The introduction was characterized by the contemporary Greek poet, Ioulios Typaldos, as "perhaps the most beautiful description ever of the political and philological situation of new Greece." Kyriakidou-Nestoros 1978: 69. It is worth mentioning that Fauriel made no differentiation between Homer's epics, Dante, Greek and Serbian ballads, and treated them as "popular poetry." Burke 1978: 20.

[21] Ibrovac 1966: 69.

[22] Ibrovac 1966: 285–286.

[23] Ibrovac 1966: 297–298.

[24] Ibrovac 1966: 305.

[25] Less known collections of Greek songs are treated marginally by Greek as well as foreign scholars. With the exception of A. Politis who briefly registers their existence, enumerating only a few of them. Politis A. 2011: 237. The only book that deals thoroughly with the problem is still, to my knowledge, Ibrovac 1966: 69–113. Some interesting details are also given by Kyriakidou-Nestoros 1978: 76–85 and Herzfeld 1982: 12–13. There are some isolated cases of travelers who in the fifteenth and sixteenth centuries made some notes on folk songs, such as Martinus Crusius (1526–1607), professor of Tübingen University who, in his *Turco-Graeciae libri octo* (p. 513, 1584), cited the first Modern Greek folk song of love (wholly accessible on: http://www.uni-mannheim.de/mateo/camenahist/autoren/crusius_hist.html [03.03.2016]). (Ibrovac 1966: 30 ff.). From the middle of the sixteenth century, there is also the well-known manuscript bought by the Ambassador of Austria in Constantinople, Augier Busbecq, and sent by him to the Imperial Library in Venice, which was discovered in 1870 by Constantine Sathas (Ibrovac 1966: 31). Before that time it belonged to Akakios, metropolitan of Naupaktos

The publication was followed by the mushrooming of similar collections in other countries in subsequent years.[26] Although Fauriel's work is a milestone in the development both of the interest in Modern Greek literature abroad, as well as in Greece itself, *Chants populaires...* also marked the beginning of – I don't hesitate to say – the inglorious tradition of approaching Greek folk songs by West European scholars by treating them similarly to the classical texts, and thus before publication emending and "adjusting" them according to the scholar prerogatives, which I shall elaborate on below.

The question of Greek folklore, its relation to the folk tradition of other European countries and its distinctive features, has been subject of many studies and was researched thoroughly, so it is obviously beyond the scope of this book to present it in detail.[27] What is worth mentioning is that in Greece, more than anywhere else in Europe, the nineteenth-century folk studies were dominated by the archaeological model (Herder's idea) based on the preference of the past over the present, which in the Greek case was obviously the classical past.[28] Secondly,

and Arta (Pernot 1931: i; Wagner 1874: ix). The subsequent editions of some parts of that manuscript were: Wagner 1874, Legrand 1874, Pernot 1931. The other attempts at publishing Greek songs had been made by Baron Werner von Haxthausen (1780–1842) in 1814 (Ibrovac 1966: 86) or Theodoros Manousis (before 1814) and Jean-Alexandre Bouchon (1821). Ibrovac 1966: 84–87; 94–95.

[26] Among others: Müller (1825), Sheridan (1825), Tomasseo (1842), Marcellus (1851), Lévy (1860), Passow (1860), Kind (1861). Greek folk songs were also very quickly translated into Polish. In 1829 in Petersburg and 1933 in Poznań, Aleksander Chodźko, the professor of Slavonic Literature at Collège de France (1857–1883) published his collection of Greek demotic songs and some paraphrases of them as *Poezye*. Another attempt was made by Józef Dunin-Borkowski, who imitated Klephtic songs in his poems. Borowska 2004: 25–31.

[27] Kyriakidou-Nestoros 1978; Herzfeld 1982; Danforth 1984; Beaton 1986.

[28] Alexiou 1984–1985: 7–9. Significantly, the nineteenth-century European scholars dealing with Greek folklore were interested in it only if it concerned the antiquity and could somehow explain some problems of Ancient Greek mythology and literature. A good example is Lawson's well-known study (Lawson 1910) that I will allude to later. Alexiou also pays attention to the fact that, within the framework of European folklore studies, Greek folklore has been marginalized. Alexiou 1984–1985: 9. Interestingly, the same contempt concerns Byzantium and its legacy. Avdikos 2010: 158. The nineteenth-century Greek intellectuals changed the perspective of seeing their ancient ancestors, now the ancient Greeks were identified with the Greeks themselves. Kyriakidou-Nestoros 1978: 45. Nikolaos Politis briefly explained his usage of the archaeological

as Alexiou convincingly writes, the Greek case was characterized by an unprecedented tendency to idealize, according to the romantic movement, folk songs as "the spontaneous creation of the eternal spirit of the nation."[29]

This attitude resulted from the same interest, visible in Western as well as in Eastern Europe, in studying folk poetry as an inextricable part of a national consciousness and national independence movements.[30] Thus, the idealization of folklore in Greece was strongly connected with politics, especially as the young country had many territorial ambitions, mainly to regain its lands in Asia Minor, which is known as the Megali Idea (Μεγάλη Ιδέα).[31] "The Great Idea" was partly a reaction against the well-known Fallmerayer's theory[32] that the contemporary Greeks have

motif in his *Study on the life of modern Greeks* (Μελέται επί του βίου των νεωτέρων Ελλήνων, vol. 2, 1871–1874): "Greek people conserved in everything the ancient Greek life" (ο ελληνικός λαός διετήρησε πολλαχού τον αρχαίον ελληνικόν βίον). Cited by Kyriakidou-Nestoros 1978: 91.

[29] Alexiou 1984–1985: 8. Interestingly, as Kyriakidou-Nestoros notes, as much as the German term Volksgeist was rather focused on the future and was strongly connected with Messianism and a belief in a special role of the German nation, in the Greek case it was orientated towards the past and the conviction that the only perfection lies in the classical antiquity. Kyriakidou-Nestoros 1978: 45. See also Herzfeld 1982: 10 ff.

[30] Beaton 2004: 4.

[31] The Megali Idea of joining all the Greek lands inhabited by the Greeks and making the "Greece of Two Continents and Five Seas" with two capitals, in Constantinople and in Athens, was present as an official ideology from 1844 until the Asia Minor catastrophe in 1922. Avdikos 2010: 158. Wrazas 2010: 57–59.

[32] It is contained in the first volume of his *Geschichte der Halbinsel Morea während des Mittelalters* (1830). The Greek scientists of that time showed a strong contradiction against Fallmerayer's theory. Most notably, Spyridon Zambelios, who in the preface to his collection of demotic songs (*Άσματα Δημοτικά της Ελλάδος. Εκδοθέντα μετά μελέτης ιστορικής περί Μεσαιωνικού Ελληνισμού*, 1952) proposed three phases of Greek history: ancient, Byzantine and modern trying to prove the continuity of Modern Greece. Another historian who attempted to put together the whole history of Modern Greece, rehabilitating the transient period of medieval Byzantium, was Constantine Paparrigopoulos in his monumental multi-volume work *History of the Greek Nation* (*Ιστορία του Ελληνικού Έθνους*, 6 volumes, 1860–1877). Kyriakidou-Nestoros 1978: 46–47. Herzfeld 1982: 39–42; 75–81. Puchner 2009: 75 ff; 133. See also Wrazas 2008: 51–67.

nothing in common with their ancient predecessors, including their language, customs and popular tradition.[33]

What was yet the most important, as I suppose, in the Greek model of folklore, was the approach to the folk song as to the written not oral text and separating it from the performative context.[34]

It is now well-known, for instance, that Passow (1860) had the tendency to conflate some variants of the songs in order to – just like the classical philologists, the editors of ancient texts, used to – create the established model text of a given song based on all accessible versions.[35] Besides this, as it turns out, most of the collections of folk songs that were published in the nineteenth century were not the reproductions of oral performances at all, but the work of a scholarly mind organizing and readjusting the text material.[36]

We can observe the same phenomenon in Politis' well-known collection (1914), where he used to correct what he thought to be not "Greek" enough, cutting out the passages he did not like and inserting his own verses.[37] I shall allude to that practice subsequently.[38]

This phenomenon has many consequences, as we shall see in particular parts of the present book, and influences not only the texts themselves but also the methods of their studying, as well as their interpretation. The constant interaction of the literate world and the folk one,

---

[33] Ibrovac 1966: 144. Avdikos 2010: 158. As Herzfeld strongly underlines, it is impossible to understand the development of Greek folklore without taking into account this ideological background. Herzfeld 1982: 7–8.

[34] Until the nineteenth century, before the first collections were published, demotic songs did not exist beyond the performative context. Beaton 1986: 110. For more on the peculiarities of the Greek case, see Puchner 2009: 73 ff.

[35] Beaton 2004: 10, 203; Politis A. 2011: 256–257.

[36] Dimaras 1987: 11. As Beaton (2004: 6–7) strongly underlines, neither Werner von Haxthausen (1780–1842), the author of the collection of Greek songs (in print 1935), nor Claude Fauriel had ever visited Greece and drew information from the educated informants from the Greek diaspora, many of them close friends of the collectors. For how the romantic movement together with Greek nationalism affected the publishing of folk songs both in Greece and abroad, see: Beaton 1986: 115; Beaton 2004: 1–12. About the rise of cultural nationalism in the South Slav Habsburg lands in the same period and the role Serbian songs played in it, see Merchiers 2007: 222–286.

[37] Alexiou 1984–1985: 7–10.

[38] The practice was nothing unusual among all the publishers and collectors of folk poetry at that time. Burke 1978: 16 ff.

mutually permeating each other, in modern Greek culture,[39] make any attempt to investigate the possible sources of any idea or the question of continuity an impossible task. These two worlds are, in the case of modern Greek literature, inseparably linked also to the Greek diglossia,[40] one the major political hot topics in the course of the nineteenth century, which makes the subject of research even less approachable. In fact, both coexisting elements: learned and popular or written and oral, as Alexiou significantly notes, make the nature of Greek tradition more diachronic and intertextual than – as was underlined throughout the nineteenth century – "continuous."[41]

A discussion about the continuity or discontinuity of Greek tradition from various points of view and according to different schools has been the subject of research since at least the late eighteenth century. This was just before the birth of the Greek state, when it became strongly ideologised by the "romantic" Philhellenic movement and generally was a result of nineteenth-century nationalist theories.[42] The debate whether Modern Greek culture in some of its manifestations is a natural descendant of its ancient predecessor or not does not seem to have ceased today, although it has definitely lost its vigour and generally, in recent scholarship, has been regarded as unconstructive.[43] The most recent approaches to the problem, especially made by Alexiou, accentuate the cyclical rather than linear aspect of time and its relation to the un-

---

[39] Alexiou 1984–1985: 16–17.

[40] There was a strong interest among Greek intellectuals from the diaspora at the beginning of the nineteenth century in the spoken language of the people. Together with the collections of folk songs, a lot of collections of Greek proverbs appeared, as well as some glossaries of the demotic language. Kyriakidou-Nestoros 1978: 62–65. Diglossia as a term in the Greek case means the coexistence of two different forms of one language: *katharevousa* (καθαρεύουσα) that belonged to the "high" educated community and *dimotiki* (δημοτική) that was used as a spoken language.

[41] Alexiou 1984–1985: 23. Beaton suggests that there are no direct literary influences at the early stage of this tradition and before the first editions of folk songs were printed probably any concept of the fixed text influenced the oral tradition. Beaton 1986: 110.

[42] Vryonis (1978: 237–256) gives a convincing survey of the theories. See also Alexiou 2002a: 8–16. As for the role folk studies played in Greece in the shaping of Greek national identity, see Politis A. 2011: 241–262. The whole passage is taken from my paper Bzinkowski 2015a: 83–84.

[43] Tziovas 2014: 9.

derstanding of what Greek culture is in modern times, and thus broaden the research perspective trying to embrace language, myth and metaphor present not only in written texts, but also in ritual manifestations of folk culture.[44] Together with the change of attitude to the question of whether the "survivalism" of ancient culture should be examined synchronically or diachronically, including the transitional phases of the Byzantine and Ottoman periods that left indelible traces on Greek culture, there was a sort of rehabilitation of the studies written mainly at the end of the nineteenth and beginning of the twentieth century. We should remember that the scholars with a classical education faced the question rather "romantically," in accordance with the ideological tendencies of their times.

The first collections that were published in Greece during the nineteenth century appeared on Corfu and were collected by members belonging to Dionysios Solomos' circle, Antonios Manousos (1850) and Spyridon Zambelios (1852).[45] It is also worth mentioning that these are the first collections of Greek songs ever that were based on field work and restricted to a particular geographical area of Greece.[46]

Their successors in the second half of the nineteenth century continued the regional collections from Cyprus (Sakellarios 1891), Pontos (Ioannidis 1870, Sathas-Legrand 1876), Crete (Jeannarakis 1876) and Epirus (Chasiotis 1866, Arvanitos 1880).[47] One should not omit the collection published a little earlier in Leipzig by Passow (1860), the first

---

[44] Alexiou 2002a; Alexiou 2002b. There is no way here to enumerate all the valuable studies devoted to the "continuity problem," however, it seems important to recall here the most significant of them, such as the classic study by Herzfeld 1982 or the most recent volume of essays by Tziovas 2014.

[45] Beaton 2004: 9. Until then it is probable that most of the demotic songs that were published in the collections had nothing in common with their oral versions.

[46] Beaton 1986: 115–116. A. Politis regards Manousos' collection as a compilation of some songs taken from Fauriel and Tomasseo with the addition of a few new songs and thus – according to him – it is groundless to call it an original one. A. Politis 2011: 252.

[47] Ibrovac 1966: 235. Beaton 1986: 116. A. Politis adds to this list a small collection by Lelekos (1852), however, it seems rather to be a compilation from different regions and not concentrated on one area. Politis A. 2011: 253. Herzfeld proves that this collection is a mixture of folk songs embroidered with references to Ancient Greek tragedy and other ancient authors, and thus should be regarded as a forgery. Herzfeld 1982: 81–86.

critical collection of Greek demotic songs, being a landmark in folk bibliography.[48]

As a matter of fact, the middle of the nineteenth century is regarded as a starting point from which any collections of Greek folk songs – composed both by Greeks and foreigners – being published are focused on regional variants and devoted to local traditions.[49]

At the end of the nineteenth century and during the first decades of the twentieth century, folklore studies in Greece were under the predominant influence of Nikolaos Politis. The father of research on Greek folk traditions in 1883 introduced the Greek term for "folklore," laografia (λαογραφία), that was officially used from 1909,[50] the year when the influential periodical *Laografia* was founded by him, and also the first year of the Greek Folklore Society (Ελληνική Λαογραφική Εταιρεία).[51] However, it was the publication of his well-known *Selections from the Songs of Greek People* (*Εκλογαί από τα τραγούδια του ελληνικού λαού*) in 1914 that became a real milestone for the next generations of folklorists, as well as for Greeks who, until now, regard it as the most authoritative point of reference, especially in school education.[52] It may sound astonishing that – although Politis' collection is composed by the methods of compilation and conflation of all collections of folk songs existing until that time – after a century it is still a valuable and, for most educated Greeks, a unique source of knowledge about Greek folk songs.[53]

The twentieth-century folklorists continued focusing on regional oral material, increasing their interest – as Beaton notes – in the performed oral text.[54] The enormous abundance of published collections

---

[48] Beaton 1986: 116. Politis A. 2011: 256–257. Ibrovac 1966: 213–214.

[49] Politis A. 2011: 257.

[50] Alexiou 1984–1985: 14. Avdikos 2010: 159. Nikolaos Politis knew he had used the term that occured in Hellenistic times in a completely different meaning, in reference to the tax the Egyptians had to pay. Kyriakidou-Nestoros 1978: 152. See also Puchner 2009: 117 ff.

[51] As for Politis' contribution to folklore studies, see especially Herzfeld 1982: 97–122.

[52] Beaton 1986: 116.

[53] For more on the comparative method of Nikolaos Politis, see the especially detailed analysis by Kyriakidou-Nestoros 1978: 99–110. See also Puchner 2009: 138.

[54] Beaton 1986: 116.

during the twentieth century makes it impossible to enumerate all the most important ones that I allude to in the present book. However, some excellent editions that are worth mentioning and which turned out to be very useful for the subject of this study were, among others: the collection by the Academy of Athens (EDT 1947), the collections of folk songs from the Mani Peninsula by Pasayanis (1928) and Kougeas (2000), the magnificent edition of *mirologia* by Saunier (1999) and from the newest Matsinopoulos' collection of songs from South-West Peloponnesus (2008) or Sklavenitis' *mirologia* from Lefkada (2012).

Nowadays, except Politis' slightly outdated selection of folk songs, there is no official and up-to-date collection encompassing all the previous regional variants of songs. It has been postulated lately that a modern corpus of demotic songs should be created, including their new classification, taking into account the diachronic aspect and different variants of a particular song to show its development or, for instance, based on thematic criteria.[55]

2. *Mirologia* and the *songs of the Underworld and Charos*

Until now, any cohesive attempt to classify demotic songs was not fully successful and there have been many different approaches according to the chosen criteria. Usually, the folklorists or researchers of oral literature do not agree with each other as regards the proposed categories. Thus, the classification taken by Politis in his *Selection...* based on fourteen groups of songs [historical (ιστορικά), klephtic (κλέφτικα), acritic (ακριτικά), ballads (παραλογές), songs of love (της αγάπης), wedding songs (νυφιάτικα), lullabies (ναναρίσματα), Christmas carols and Easter songs (κάλανδα, βαΐτικα), exile songs (της ξενιτιάς), dirges – *mirologia* (μοιρολόγια), *mirologia* of the Underworld and Charos (μοιρολόγια του Κάτω Κόσμου και του Χάρου), gnomic songs (γνωμικά), work and country (Vlachic) songs (εργατικά και βλάχικα), and satirical

[55] Politis A. 2011: 323–340. First published as a paper in the periodical *Ariadni*, t. 9, Rethymno 2003, 181–188.

(περιγελαστικά)], is commonly accepted, but if we compare it with the other ways of classification, it differs significantly.[56]

Without entering into detail concerning the question of the classification of demotic songs, especially as it is not the subject of the present book and will not be helpful in my investigation of the personality of Charos, it is worth underlining here that, from all the above-mentioned groups, the *mirologia* (funeral laments, dirges) constitute a separate group characterized by unquestionable uniqueness and lyricism.[57]

The *mirologia* songs and, generally, the ritual aspects of death and of lament songs, as well as their socio-cultural context, have been subject of countless studies, in particular those by Alexiou (1974),[58] Danforth (1982), Seremetakis (1991), Gail Holst-Warhaft (1992), Saunier (1999), Psychogiou (2008) and lately Håland (2014).

As Alexiou proves using historical and linguistic analysis of the term, *mirologia* (μοιρολόγια) have their origin in the word *moira* (μοῖρα) and, according to her, probably some phrases known even from the Homeric poems, such as *moiran lego/katalego* (μοῖραν λέγω/καταλέγω), gained a new meaning, when simultaneously Moira became a goddess responsible for man's death. What initially meant "song to fate" changed its meaning into "lament song" because of the confusion concerning the terms *myromai* (μύρομαι) and *moira*. According to her, the term *mirolo-*

---

56 For instance, Stilpnon Kyriakidis' well-known classification is based on general criteria and contains two groups of songs: narrative (διηγηματικά) and proper songs (κυρίως άσματα). Politis A. 2011: 327. Kyriakidis, although he opposed Politis for his archaeological method and wanted to distance himself from the historical methodology in favour of functionalism, in fact he failed, accepting the idea of continuity. Avdikos 2010: 163. On Kyriakidis, see especially the thorough analysis by Kyriakidou-Nestoros 1978: 111–147. Guy Saunier's classification is based on chronological distinction. He divided the songs according to the thematic content as: archaic, old, newer, recent and modern. Politis A. 2011: 53–54. Dimaras divides folk songs into three main categories: 1. songs related to human life (που αναφέρονται στην ανθρώπινη ζωή), 2. historical songs (ιστορικά), 3. ballads (παραλογές). Dimaras 1987: 9–10.

57 Borowska 2008: 78. It has been noted that the Greek villagers usually do not classify dirges as songs (τραγούδια). Herzfeld 1982: 45.

58 In the course of the book, I allude to the second edition revised by D. Yatromanolakis and P. Roilos, published in 2002. Here I mention only some of them, the most important ones, with the other ones appearing in the subsequent parts of the present study.

gi is thus deeply rooted in antiquity and, at least from the Hellenistic times, has been used in the modern meaning.[59]

It is noteworthy that the term *mirologi* is general and may encompass different groups of songs relating to, among others, departure from home, those leaving their country or changing their religion and marry.[60] The *mirologia* for the dead, which constitute some of the material of the present study, are the laments sung by women by the coffin as well as the tomb.[61] They are improvised by professional mourners, using the techniques of oral formulas and an organized compositional scheme and usually praise the dead in the third person, address the dead by their name or take a form of long dialogues.[62] In some cases, it is the dead speaking about their death and present condition in the Underworld. *Mirologia* cultivated in the Mani, the region where they are extremely popular, have a special character.[63] The songs sung not in the common fifteen-syllable "political verse" are different in character in comparison with other Greek dirges and contain a lot of details concerning the life of the dead.[64]

As I have already mentioned, Nikolaos Politis specified a special group of *mirologia* that he called "*mirologia* of the Underworld and Charos" (μοιρολόγια του Κάτω Κόσμου και του Χάρου) treating them as a separate category not only of *mirologia* but also of all songs. Politis rightly felt that the songs are different from the rest of *mirologia*, but did not have any idea how to classify them due to the fact that they allude as well as the other lament songs to the eschatological sphere, although in a completely different way. They very rarely contain any allusions to the particular dead, it is Charos that plays the main role in them and they usually have a narrative character. They have a lot of common features with the songs belonging to the acritic cycle – especially those related to the death of Digenis – or the long narrative ballads. As Alexiou adds,

---

[59] Alexiou 2002b: 110–118. As for the explanation of the term, see also Hutter, Sike: 1979: 59.

[60] Alexiou 2002b: 118–119.

[61] Politis A. 2011: 32–33. Hutter, Sikke 1979: 59.

[62] Alexiou 2002b: 122–124.

[63] Politis A. 2011: 33. Hutter, Sikke 1979: 60.

[64] Politis L. 1973: 87.

some fragments of such long compositions might have been assimilated into more recent ritual laments.[65]

It is noteworthy that the figure of Charos generally does not play a significant role in *mirologia* and does not appear in most of the songs. Thus, it would not be groundless to think that, perhaps, originally he might have belonged to another group of songs and was later adapted by *mirologia* and absorbed, mostly as a synonym to personified death as well as the ruler of the Underworld, by folk imagination and became a component of ritual laments. The problem, obviously, is highly complicated due to the fact that we do not possess, with some extremely rare exceptions I have already alluded to, the texts of demotic songs older than the nineteenth-century collections.

Nikolaos Politis' idea that the songs of Charos should be approached differently was not his invention, but it also appeared in older collections of folk songs both of foreign and Greek authors.

In Passow's *Popularia carmina Graeciae recentioris* (1860) we find a group of *mirologia* (*Myrologia. Carmina composita a feminis mortem propinqui lugentibus*, pp. 257–288) as well as songs he entitled *Ο Χάρος* (*Carmina quibus Charon omnes mortales superans describitur*, pp. 289–310). Similarly, Chasiotis in his collection of demotic songs from Epirus (1866) differentiates these two groups, giving them the titles *Του Χάρου* (pp. 167–171) and *Μυρολόγια* (pp. 172–185), although in this group he incorporates, for instance, a song entitled by him *Of Charos and of Earth* (*Του Χάρου και της γης*, p. 180).

Bernhard Schmidt in his well-known collection of folk songs translated into German, *Griechische märchen, sagen und volkslieder* (1877) follows the same scheme, classifying separately *Myrológia im engeren Sinne. Eigentliche Klagenlieder* (pp. 150–159) and *Lieder von Charos und der Unterwelt* (pp. 158–181).

Twentieth-century collectors generally continued such a classification, separating the songs of Charos from the rest of *mirologia*, with some peculiarities. In the Ioannou collection (1966), *The Songs of Charos* (*Για το Χάρο*, pp. 387–141) follow the *Dirges for the Dead and Their Fate* (*Θρήνοι για το νεκρό και τη μοίρα του*, pp. 323–369) and precede

[65] Alexiou 2002b: 126.

the songs he classifies as a separate group of *mirologia* as *Of the Underworld* (*Για τον Κάτω Κόσμο*, pp. 415–451). Petropoulos in his second volume of *Greek Demotic Songs* (*Ελληνικά δημοτικά τραγούδια, τ. Β'*, 1958–1959) entitles the whole group *Mirologia* and songs of Charos (Μοιρολόγια και τραγούδια του Χάρου) differentiating the following subgroups: 1. Dirges for the dead, dialogues (Θρήνοι για το νεκρό, διάλογοι), 2. *Mirologia* for particular persons (Μοιρολόγια για ορισμένα προσώπα), 3. Laments of the dead for departing, for the horrors of Hades (Οδυρμοί του νεκρού για το χωρισμό, για του Άδη τα δεινά), 4. Allegories, similes (Αλληγορίες, παρομοιώσεις), 5. Of Charos (Του Χάρου), 6. *Mirologia* from Mani (Μοιρολόγια της Μάνης). Theros (1952) distinguishes three categories: 1. Songs of Charos (Χαροντικά), 2. *Mirologia* from everywhere (Μοιρολόγια από παντού), 3. *Mirologia* from Mani (Μανιάτικα μοιρολόγια).

In more recent collections of *mirologia,* the tendency to use more elaborate categorization continues.[66] Matsinopoulos, for instance, proposes in his collection of *mirologia* from Trifylia in South-West Peloponessos (2008) the following classification, based on six subgroups: 1. Of departing and farewell (Του Αποχωρισμού-Αποχαιρετισμού), 2. Of solitude of the house (Της μοναξιάς του σπιτιού), 3. Of memorials and the grave (Των μνημοσύνων και του τάφου), 4. Of Charos and Charissa (Του Χάρου και της Χάρισσας), 5. Of the Underworld (Για τον Κάτου Κόσμο), 6. Different *mirologia* (Μοιρολόγια διάφορα, μη άλλως ταξινομούμενα).

In some cases, the attempts of the collectors seem odd at first sight and not quite understandable, like in Sklavenitis' collection from Lefkada (2012), where he distinguishes from the rest of *mirologia* the songs "of housewife" (της νοικοκυράς) and "of mother" (της μάνας), placing the songs of Charos among the other non-categorized group.

As we have seen from the above survey of the *songs of the Underworld and Charos* and their place in the corpus of demotic songs, there is a lot of confusion and uncertainty as to where exactly they should belong.

---

[66] An interesting simple attempt at categorization can be found, among others, in a French paper, where the authors propose three groups of *mirologia*: adapted to the age of the deceased, more personal ones and, lastly, the songs of Charos (in their paper always as "Charon"). Hutter, Sikke 1979: 59.

Remarkably, the figure of Charos may appear in every group of *mirologia*, not necessarily in the class of songs restricted to him. Thus, in order to attempt to sketch any convincing characteristics of this enigmatic and ambiguous person belonging to folk mythology, it is indispensable to use the whole range of *mirologia* in which he appears, in some specific cases also including the songs not categorized exactly as lament songs or the *songs of the Underworld and Charos*, but, for instance, also acritic songs, where a well-known motif of fighting with Charos-Death appears, which I ventured to do in the present book.[67]

It is also extremely important to underline the fact that, due to objective reasons, the research of the songs of Charos cannot take into account the diachronic aspect of folk tradition. There is no possibility, besides some sparse exceptions,[68] to trace the development of demotic songs before the nineteenth century. Thus the chronological aspect of approaching the songs in which the figure of Charos appears is rather excluded. That, of course, does not mean that they do not contain any features indicating their older origin, nor that some characteristics do not betray earlier cultural layers, especially concerning the imagery and mythological aspect, which I also attempt to elucidate in my investigation of the enigmatic figure of Charos in demotic songs.

---

[67] Due to the abundance of others sources belonging to folk literature in which the figure of Charos appears, especially folk tales, I decided to confine myself only to demotic poetry. The other reason for excluding the Charos of folk tales in the present book is that his person, in most cases, generally differs a lot as regards the characteristics of his image occurring in folk songs.

[68] The earliest folk songs we have are two manuscripts with the song of Armouris, one from the fifteenth century, the other dated 1461. From that time until the end of the Ottoman period in the early nineteenth century, the evidence we possess, except Bouvier's seventeenth-century manuscript I have already mentioned, is very scarce. Beaton 2004: 82–86. Significantly, it is impossible to decide when most of the folk songs, regardless of their origin, collected in the nineteenth century were composed. Burke 1978: 21.

Chapter II

REPRESENTATIONS

1. The Underworld of demotic songs

In the eleventh book of the *Odyssey*, Achilles' surprised *psyche* asks Odysseus: "How didst thou dare to come down to Hades, where dwell the unheeding dead, the phantoms of men outworn" (πῶς ἔτλης Ἄϊδόσδε κατελθέμεν, ἔνθα τε νεκροὶ/ ἀφραδέες ναίουσι, βροτῶν εἴδωλα καμόντων, Od. 11, 474–476).[69] Achilles' speech expresses more about the condition of human afterlife existence in Homeric poems than any other fragment in both epic stories. The hero, unconquered in the Trojan War and now deprived – as any other ghost in Hades – of conscience and memories before drinking a drop of blood, disillusions his interlocutor as to the merits of death. He would prefer to be "the hireling of another" and live a modest and poor life rather than "to be lord over all the dead that have perished" (βουλοίμην κ' ἐπάρουρος ἐὼν θητευέμεν ἄλλῳ,/ ἀνδρὶ παρ' ἀκλήρῳ, ᾧ μὴ βίοτος πολὺς εἴη,/ ἢ πᾶσιν νεκύεσσι καταφθιμένοισιν ἀνάσσειν, Od., 489–491). In fact, in Homeric poems the vision of the afterlife of an individual is completely hopeless because, according to archaic Greek representations, the world of the dead is not a place of punishment, nor reward, as it is in later Greek eschatology. At this early stage of Greek thought, human souls are just shades of the living wandering aimlessly on the asphodel meadows through the darkness of

[69] Homer, *The Odyssey* with an English Translation by A.T. Murray, text accessible on: http://www.perseus.tufts.edu/ [17.04.2017]. The present chapter is a shortened version of my paper: Bzinkowski 2011b.

the lower world.[70] However, an attempt to see a coherent eschatological system in a poetic vision is an arduous task, as the elements constituting the afterlife of an individual are not only veiled and incoherent but, in most cases, even exclude each other. Still, we are not able to discern if the epic vision reflects the popular eschatological beliefs of the people living in the archaic period and earlier, or if it is just a poetic concept devoid of convincing parallels in reality.[71]

Nevertheless, such a sullen and gloomy lot of every man is not a Hellenic nor Homer's idea, but contains traces of archaic thinking. If we closely compare similar ancient epic texts from the Middle East, we will find the same obscurity of the eschatological vision as well as the same beliefs regarding the afterlife of an individual. For instance, in the epic of Gilgamesh, the story known among the Sumerians and later adopted by Akkadians, the Netherworld (known as Irkalla, Aralu or Kigal) is depicted as a "house of dust and darkness" whose inhabitants eat clay and are clothed in bird feathers.[72] In another myth, one of the most famous ever, about the descent of Inanna (Assyrian Ishtar) into the Underworld, the formula significantly underlining the conditions of those who dwell in the darkness of the Netherworld appears: "Don't let your precious metal be alloyed there with the dirt of the Underworld."[73] The element of "dust," "dirt" and "clay" is also a characteristic of the conception of Sheol, the earliest notion of the afterlife in Jewish Scriptures, in Greek translations of the Bible rendered always as "Hades"[74] – the term that has a long-established tradition in the Christian religious texts, including both Testaments in which it occurs in the sense of "abyss," "a bottomless

[70] I use alternatively the following English synonyms for "the abode of the dead," namely for the place where the "soul" is believed to go after death: the Underworld, the world below, the Netherworld, the lower world, the other world. They correspond in a way with Modern Greek equivalents.

[71] Sourvinou-Inwood 1995: 107.

[72] *Zaświaty*... 1999: 65–66; Bernstein 2006: 20.

[73] English translation is available on: http://www.piney.com/InanasDescNether.html [17.04.2017].

[74] I mean here the Koine Greek version of the Bible translated between the third and second century BC in Alexandria, known as the Septuagint. The New Testament authors continued this method, thus joining the Jewish and Greek tradition. See Bernstein 2006: 171. Tromp 1969: 85–91.

pit" and thus of "Hell" itself.[75] Like the Homeric Underworld, Sheol is a place for everyone, regardless of life's deeds, it is morally neutral, exactly like the Babylonian lower world.[76] The difference between the two traditions is visible in the characteristics of the world below. In Jewish tradition, Sheol is described as an abyss in which all the dead, now being merely weak shadows exactly like in Homeric poems, end up. Often it is compared to a cistern, a water basin or a well[77] and thus the concept seems to underline rather the cavity of the Underworld, depicted as an indeterminate hole. Anyhow, the concept of "neutral death," according to which all the dead remain in half-life without reward or punishment, had developed long before the Homeric poems were composed and had been handed down in oral tradition. From the Mesopotamia of the 3rd Millennium before Christ, the concept permeated into classical antiquity through the Persian culture.[78] The later idea of "moral death" developed in Greek colonies in Sicily under the influence of Pythagoras and was passed on to Greece.

---

[75] Anagnostopoulos 1984: 269–274, where he provides in the references a detailed list of occurrences of the word "Hades" in the Old and the New Testament. For more on the conception of the Beyond in the Old Testament in comparison with other ancient Semitic texts, see detailed studies by Tromp 1969 or Johnston 2010. According to them, the word "Sheol" more frequently occurs in poetical and wisdom literature, such as Psalms, Proverbs etc., than in historical books. Moreover, we don't know how the term is related to the Accadian word "hursan," meaning "the place of ordeal," nor when it was introduced in Israel or if the Israelites had the conscience of its original meaning. Tromp 1969: 21–23. It is also worth noticing that the Israelites were rather not interested in the afterlife beliefs and concentrated more on their relation with Jahwe in the present rather than on speculation about life after death. See Johnston 2010: 83–84.

[76] There is no detailed and coherent representation of Sheol in Testament literature and an attempt to reconstruct it is difficult because of the language by which it is described. See Bernstein 2006: 171; *Zaświaty…* 1999: 213–214. The scenery of Sheol in the Old Testament, except the all-surrounding darkness as a dominating feature, also encompasses such elements as: impetuous rivers, the border mountains, the desert, the ocean. See Tromp 1969: 129–151; Johnston 2010: 85 ff.

[77] Bernstein 2006: 174, cites the idiom *jôrdê bôr*, which means "these who descend to the grave" – a metaphorical expression for "to die." The word *bôr* has associations with a pit, a hole, a cistern or even a dungeon. In many Psalms the dead are regarded "to have descended to the cistern" (Ps. 28, 1; 88, 5; 143, 7). See *Zaświaty…* 1999: 213.

[78] Bernstein 2006: 15–16.

One of the main features of folk culture is "double-faith," in other words a harmonic coexistence of pagan beliefs with Christianity.[79] In the case of Greece, as attested by ethnographic material gathered in rural societies, especially in the nineteenth century, we are dealing with the world of Christian beliefs, namely the legacy of the Byzantine church on one hand, and, on the other, Greek-Roman elements deeply rooted in the Hellenic ground since ancient times.[80] These two parallel worlds that mostly used to exclude each other – similarly to the two languages that were used throughout centuries: the learned and the spoken Greek – still coexist in demotic songs, which I shall show subsequently.

The Underworld, according to the most archaic ideas concerning the cosmological picture, is situated at the lowest of the three levels of the world, below the earth and the highest level, the sky.[81] Such a tripartite image characteristic of the Indo-European vision of the world preserved in the Christian concept of the New Testament is, however, influenced by ethic valuation – the Underworld becomes a place under the power of Satan and is described as a place of punishment and suffering of the souls of the dead.[82] Anyhow, we deal here with the vision of the world of the dead within a pair of oppositions – down/up and the Underworld/the sky.[83] Folk culture, regardless of the Christian vision of the world that inevitably dominated the pagan one, retained the pre-Christian concepts concerning the place where the soul heads after death. If, for instance, we look at Russian lament songs, the destination of the soul is completely uncertain and obscure, which is reflected in the names of that place: in the Old Russian beliefs it is *bezvestnoje, nevedomaja strana*

---

[79] The first time the term *dvoviria* (*двовір'я*) was used by Thedosius of Kiev (Феодосий Печерский) with reference to the process of peacefully coexisting elements of Christian and pagan beliefs in the conscience of Russians. See Riasanovsky 2005: 28. The "double-faith" is by no means original for Greek folklore, it is common to all areas inhabited by Slavic peoples and is vital especially among the Eastern Slavs. See Strimska 2005: 209–215.

[80] As for the coexistence of the elements of Antiquity and Christianity in Byzantium see Constantelos 1966. An interesting excerpt: Byzantine and Ancient Greek Religiosity is accessible on: http://www.myriobiblos.gr/texts/english/Constantelos_3.html [11.05.2017].

[81] *Słownik stereotypów i symboli ludowych*, t. I, 2, 1999: 465.

[82] *Słownik stereotypów i symboli ludowych*, t. I, 2, 1999: 466.

[83] Bylina 1999: 20.

(unknown land) or *čužaja strana* (strange land)[84] and similarly the road waiting for the dead is unknown and distant. In one of the dirges, the soul of a newly dead girl is described as soaring *za oblački, za chodiačcii, k krasnu solnyšku* (beyond the clouds, beyond the known paths, into the beautiful sky). In many languages, there is a widespread occurrence of the name of the place where the soul goes after death connected with the folk belief that it constitutes a parallel world, situated somehow in opposition to *this world* and thus dividing the dead from the living. It is usually called *the other world, that world*, like in Polish – *tamten świat, drugi świat*[85] or Macedonian *onoj svet* (*оној свет*) as an opposition to *this world – ovoj svet* (*овој свет*).[86]

The Greek other world is more specific, which is confirmed by the names that in a way preserve, as I have already remarked, the archaic ideas concerning the afterlife beliefs. One of the most common names of the world of the dead in Greek demotic songs is still the Ancient Greek "Hades" (ο Άδης), now meaning only a place, not the God of the Underworld, depicted as sunless (ανήλιαγος) and absorbing all the dead regardless of their deeds in life. This eschatological concept of "neutral death," as I mentioned above, has nothing in common with Christian beliefs as there is no hope for a man who is just a prisoner and shares

---

[84] Bylina 1999: 14 f. The reconstruction of the pre-Christian Slavic beliefs concerning the place where the souls of the dead were gathered is an arduous task. The conclusions resulting from the research do not allow us to think that there was one dominant Pan-Slavic belief regarding the afterlife. Among many theories, we can suppose that the other world was situated probably beyond the waters dividing the two worlds and later was called Nawie (old slav. **navъ*) meaning "dead" or "the world of the dead." There is also a well-known archaic Slavic belief that the souls were pastured on a meadow by the God of the Underworld, among others, and fertility, Veles (*Velesъ, Volosъ bogъ*). See Szyjewski 2003: 76 f.; 206 f.

[85] Przymuszała 1999: 107. The most common synonyms of the verb "to die" include in Polish the component of "the other world": *pojechać na drugi świat, pójść na tamten świat* (go to the other world, go to that world).

[86] Zadrożyńska, Vražinovski 2002: 58, who describe the funeral rites in the village Jablanica in Macedonia. While carrying out the dead from the house, the housekeeper puts for a while a piece of bread at the feet in the coffin and later treats all the members of the household to it. It is believed that this piece of bread is "for the soul of the dead so that he would not miss it in the other world" (*za duša na umreniot da mu se najt na onoj svet*).

the lot of all the dead.[87] Such a vision, analogous to Ancient Greek representations and ideas concerning the afterlife, especially in the Homeric epic, permeates all Modern Greek folk songs and is very rarely completed by the elements of Christian beliefs.[88]

According to folk belief, as we read in one of the folk songs, the Lord has created the world and has ornamented it, however, he did not equip it with three significant things: a bridge over the sea, the chance to return from Hades and a ladder to Heaven:

> Ο Κύριος έκαμε τη γη κ' εστόλισε τον κόσμον
> μα μόνο τρία πράματα δεν έπεμψε στον κόσμο·
> γιοφύριν εις τη θάλασσα και γαγερμό 'ς τον Νάδη
> και σκάλαν εις τον ουρανό να πχαίνου να γαγέρνου. (Politis 176)
> *The Lord created the earth and ornamented the world*
> *yet he did not send to the world three things*
> *a bridge over the sea, a return from Hades*
> *and a ladder to Heaven, so that people could go to and fro.*[89]

Although there is a sort of ladder or stairs (η σκάλα) to the Underworld, it is obviously a road of no return – the idea that reiterates in many lament songs, like in this one, where a mother tries to dissuade her daughter – who is certainly about to die soon – from going down the stairs because she would never come back:

> Παρακαλώ σε, κόρη μου, τη σκάλα μη κατέβης,
> γιατί σαν τήνε κατεβής, δεν θα την ξανανέβης. (EDT 168)
> *I beg you, my daughter, don't descend the stairs,*
> *because if you go down, you will never go out again.*

According to the dualist and, we could even say, vertical, folk worldview, the place of the dead is a somehow reflected picture of the world above that resounds in other Modern Greek names of the place, such as: ο Κάτω Κόσμος (the world below or the Underworld) or ο Κάτω Γης (the earth below, the under earth). The road of all the living leads to Hades, which is simply described as "πικρός" (bitter) – one of the key words used to characterize the Modern Greek Underworld (EDT 146),

---

[87] Mavrogordato 1955: 43. Borowska 2008: 78.

[88] Anagnostopoulos 1984: 269–271. He also gives a solid analysis of Christian motives in demotic poetry, see p. 320f. See also Dawkins 1942: 145–147.

[89] All translations from Modern Greek into English are by the author.

reflecting not only the popular beliefs concerning the conditions of afterlife existence, but rather the feeling of the living after bereavement, like in this song, where a mother complains to her dead child:

Εσύ, παιδί μου, εκίνησες να πας 'ς τον Κάτου κόσμο,
Κι' αφήσες τη μαννούλα σου πικρή, χαροκαμένη. (Politis 199)
You, my child, you set out to go to the Underworld,
and you left your mother bitter and bereaved.[90]

The dead long for the upper world which they had been forever deprived of; sometimes they would like to go up there (να' ρθουν στον Πάνω κόσμο, EDT 134) like in the touching conversation between Charos-Death and a young girl who says:

μόν' με πονεί οχ το σπίτι μου και οχ τον Απάνω κόσμο. (Politis 221)
Only I deeply miss my home and the World Above.

The most common phrase used as a synonym of "to die" is πάω στον Κάτω Κόσμο (I go to the world below, Politis 199, 204, 205). In one well-known dirge, we come across a comparison of a child or a bride to the little bird (πουλάκι) lost forever because she has gone to the world below:

Εχτές προχτές επέρασε να πάει 'ς τον Κάτου Κόσμο (Politis 204)
Yesterday, the day before yesterday he passed to go to the World Below.

The vision of the afterlife existence in Modern Greek Hades that dominates in demotic songs is sullen and depressive, it resounds with the imagery of the Babylonian kingdom of the dead. There is no specific landscape of the world below, the place is far from defined in a detailed depiction. The language describing the afterlife reality is very plain and simple, it is said that the deceased are just under the gravestone, under the soil, eating dust (κουρνιαχτός),[91] which is called "the poison of the gravestone" (της πλάκας το φαρμάκι):

---

[90] Interestingly, the adjective *charokamenos* (χαροκαμένος) used here is related to Charos and literally means "burnt by Charos" and thus its meaning is "bereaved," of those whose relative or friend has just died.

[91] I would daresay that the meaning of κουρνιαχτός could be extended to "ashes." In such a case, it would be an echo of a well-known connection between ashes and dying. In Polish lament songs there is a phrase equivalent to "to die" – "to go to the death ashes" (*idę w śmiertelne popioły*) which could be – as I suppose – a far echo of the pre-Christian

Στον κάτου κόσμου βρίσκονται, στην πλάκα και στο χώμα
και γεύονται τον κουρνιαχτό, της πλάκας το φαρμάκι. (EDT 163)[92]
They are at the World Below, in the grave and in soil
and they taste dust, the poison of the gravestone.

The idea of placing the world of the dead at the bottom of the vertical structure of the world, according to the folk world view, is expressed in another name for the Underworld – τα Τάρταρα – which, beyond all doubt, echoes the Ancient Greek Tartarus.[93] However, in demotic songs it is not simply a name, but a component of the phrase κάτω στα Τάρταρα της γης (down at the furthest edges of the earth), which is invariably the first part of the verse whereas the other one is replaceable. Let us look at examples of the formula with a different second component:

Κάτω στα Τάρταρα της γης, κάτω στον Κατουκόσμο (Pasayanis 51)
Down at the furthest edges of the earth, in the Underworld.

Κάτου στα Τάρταρα της γης, τα κρυοπαγωμένα (Politis 207)
Down at the furthest edges of the earth, the frozen ones.

The picture of a sort of "distorted" world of the dead is also echoed in the periphrastic names which evoke the idea of "negation" or "denial" (της Άρνης, της Αρνησιάς), where the dead sleep on the ground and have soil instead of sheets:

θα πάω 'ς της Άρνης τα βουνά, 'ς της Αρνεσιάς τη βρύση
και έχω της γης για στρώματα, σεντόνια έχω το χώμα (Politis 185)
I will go to the mountains of Denial, the founts of Denial
the earth will be a mattress for me, the soil a bed-sheet.

"The Mountains of Negation/Denial" (άρνης βουνά) that we come across here become, in different variations of the same idea, "fields" or "places" of negation (αρνησιάς μέρη/κάμποι)[94] as well as "gorges," "dales" (λαγκάδια, Politis 184; Pasayanis 15; 17), or "springs" (βρύση, Politis 233). The world below is a negation of the world above, for here "the

custom of burning corpses. See *Słownik stereotypów i symboli ludowych*, t. I, 1 1996: pp. 329–338.

92 See also Politis: 185 with the same formula slightly modified: και γεύομαι τον κουρνιαχτό, δειπνάω από το χώμα,/ και πίνω τ'ωριοστάλαχτο της πλάκας το φαρμάκι.

93 See Hesiod, Theog. 722–726. πελώρης ἔσχατα γαίης (731). See also Hom. Il. VIII, 13–16. βάθιστον ὑπὸ χθονός ἐστι βέρεθρον (14).

94 Anagnostopoulos 1984: 270.

white ones become black" (οι άσπροι μαύροι γίνονται, Pasayanis 12) and the dead, though they were close friends, seem to not recognize each other at all, "deny" (αρνιούνται) each other,[95] like in this lament song, where a mother and her child negate each other:

> Πήγα 'ς της Άρνης τα βουνά, 'ς της Άρνης τα λαγγκάδια,
> π' αρνιέται η μάννα το παιδί, και το παιδί τη μάννα,
> π' αρνειώνται και ταντρόγυνα και πλιά δεν ανταμώνουν. (Politis 184)
> *I went to the mountains of Denial, to the ravines of Denial,*
> *where a mother denies her child and a child its mother,*
> *where couples no longer meet each other.*

Thus, the folk picture of the Underworld that emerges from Modern Greek dirges evokes the idea of oblivion deeply rooted in the eschatological beliefs of many European traditions, bringing to mind once more the archaic way of conceptualizing the Netherworld we find in the Homeric depiction of Hades, where the souls are deprived of conscience before they bring a drop of blood. According to this belief, a man after death plunges into forgetfulness, which can be understood in two ways: he loses the bonds with the previous life or he is forgotten by the living. Such a conviction is attested to by another group of names of the Modern Greek Underworld, resembling the Ancient Greek river of forgetfulness, Lethe (Λήθη), the waters of which allowed the dead to forget their memories from life.[96] The variety of names following this idea circles around the semantic field of "oblivion," "forgetfulness" (λησμονιά, αλησμονιά, αλησμόνη).

There is a significant lament song, where a child addresses his/her father, asking him if he sees "that mountain over there that is the highest of all" (εκείνο το βουνό, π'άλλο ψηλό δεν ένοι) – the formula recurring in countless songs, especially ones about Charos. The description of the landscape that follows brings the idea of the passage into the Underworld through oblivion. At the foot of the mountain there is a cold spring from which the sheep drink and forget about their lambs, their

---

[95] Dawkins 1942: 143.

[96] The memory of a "border water" was quite long alive among the Eastern Slavs. In Russian folklore it is preserved in the significant name of the mythic river – *zabyt' reka* (the river of oblivion) – the dead, after crossing it, forget about the world. The water was both the border and the junction – it allowed the communication between the living and the dead. See Bylina 1999: 16–17.

flocks and the world. The father also drank from the same spring and forgot about his children and his empty house:

Το πίνουν άγρια πρόβατα κι' αλησμονάν τη στρούγκα,
το πίνουν και τα ήμερα κι' αλησμονάν τον κόσμο.
Το 'πιες και συ, πατέρα μου, και δεν ξαναθυμάσαι
και δε θυμάσαι τα παιδιά, το έρημο το σπίτι. (EDT 167)
It is drunk by wild sheep and they forget about their flock,
it is drunk by livestock and they forget about the world.
It was drunk by you, my father, and you no longer remember
you don't remember your children, your desolate house.

Moreover, according to Greek phraseology the dead are "locked down in Oblivion" where they are given keys while entering but not while they are trying to go out, where the houses are dark, the walls are covered by cobwebs[97] and all the people are mingled together, which is illustrated by this lament song of a mother and her dead daughter:

Κόρη μου, σε κλειδώσανε κάτω 'ς την Αλησμόνη
Που 'ς το μπα δίγουν τα κλειδιά, 'ς το έβγα δεν τα δίγουν [...]
Εκεί 'ν' τα σπίτια σκοτεινά, οι τοίχοι ραχνιασμένοι,
Εκεί μεγάλοι και μικροί είν' ανακατεμένοι. (Politis 206)
My daughter, you have been locked down in Oblivion,
where, if you enter you are given the keys, while you go out they are not [...]
There the houses are obscure, the walls cobwebbed,
there the significant and the insignificant ones are mixed up.

The motif of cobwebs as characteristic elements of the landscape of the realm of the dead appears in another commonly used periphrastic name of the Modern Greek Underworld, αραχνιασμένη πλάκα (cobwebbed gravestone) or αραχνιασμένη πέτρα (cobwebbed stone).[98] Such

---

[97] Mavrogordato 1955: 46 cites a conventional phrase used to describe the tombs that we come across among others in "Erotokritos," a romance written in the Cretan dialect in the early seventeenth century – Αραχνιασμένες Πόρτες (cobwebbed doors).

[98] According to the folk view of the world, especially in Slavic folk tradition, the stones are situated on the borders of the worlds, far from the places inhabited by men. They symbolize, among others, the centre of the world or the place of passage from one to another state/world. There was also a common belief that the souls of men could incarnate into the stones and, as a result, people put them onto the graves. The same applies to the marbles referring to the other world and connected inseparably with the graves. See *Słownik stereotypów i symboli ludowych*, t. I, 1, 1996: pp. 349, 438. Polish lament songs have a frequent motif of a large stone, a grave boulder – *głaz grobowy*, for instance: *Żegnam was mili przyjaciele, mnie czas pod głaz grobowy ściele* (I say farewell

expressions in most cases follow another representation of the Underworld, deeply rooted in folk conscience, namely the visualization of a funeral as a conviction that we all are eaten by "the black earth" (η μαύρη γη).[99] Both names are connected together in a commonly met formula recurring in countless versions throughout demotic poetry: μαύρη γη τσ' αραχλιασμένη πλάκα (EDT 137). Charos significantly introduces himself to a girl who is afraid of opening the door to him: "I am the son of the black earth and cobwebbed stone" (είμαι γιος της μαύρης γης τσ' αραχνιασμένης πέτρας, EDT 152). In another song it is said that Charos "throws the dead one into the black earth" ('ς τη μαύρη γης με ρήχνει, Politis 220).

According to the folk view of the world, the earth (η γη) is conceived in a very archaic way, as a mother that gives life and into which life comes back after death.[100] For bearers of traditional culture, the man is regarded as the son of the earth for whom it is his mother that gives him peace after death.[101] However, such an attitude is sometimes ambiguous and the earth is considered as a sort of divine power, a goddess that receives a man as its food,[102] which finds its reflection in various dirges

---

to you my dear friends, when time is making my bed under the grave boulder). See *Słownik stereotypów i symboli ludowych*, t. I, 1, 1996: pp. 401–403.

[99] About the relationship between the men and the earth in Greek folk tradition, see especially Alexiou 2002b: 195f. Danforth 1982: 102f., following Lawson 1910: 388, also cites an interesting curse "μη σε χωνέψει η γη" (may the earth not digest you).

[100] *Słownik stereotypów i symboli ludowych*, t. I, 2, 1999: pp. 17–36. Let me quote a fragment of a Polish lament song that gives an illustration of this conviction: *Powracasz w ziemie, co matką twą była, teraz cię strawi, niedawno żywiła* (You come back to earth that was your mother, she will digest you now, she has fed you so far). See *Słownik stereotypów i symboli ludowych*, t. I, 2, 1999: p. 35. Interestingly, we find almost the same phraseology in a Cretan phrase that should be uttered shortly three times after death, as Danforth notes: τούτ' η γης που σ' έθρεψε, τούτη θα σε φάει (This very earth which nourished you will eat you as well), see Danforth 1982: 102.

[101] *Słownik stereotypów i symboli ludowych*, t. I, 2, 1999: p. 19 f.

[102] Psychogiou 2008 in her well documented and extensive study about the rituals of death and life in Modern Greek folklore regards the periphrastic name μαύρη γη as a goddess Μαυρηγή, the divinity more powerful than death itself in the personification of Charos, whom she considers just a guide of the dead (νεκροπομπός). Psychogiou analyses the personality of the all-embracing Μαυρηγή referring to the myth of "beautiful Helen" (της 'ωραίας' Ελένης) as a vegetation goddess of death and rebirth. See Psychogiou 2008: 26 f.

where the living, though they know it is the natural course of life, complain about the fact that the earth eats everything around, both the birds and the men:

που τρώγει αιτούς και σταυραϊτούς, και νιαις με τα στολίδια
τρώει του μαννάδων τα παιδιά, τουν αδερφιών ταδέρφια,
που τρώγει και τα αντρόγυνα τα πολυαγαπήμενα. (Politis 175)
that eats the eagles and small eagles, young girls with ornaments,
that eats children from mothers, brothers from sisters,
that eats the couples that loved each other so much.

Another lament song introduces a dramatic monologue of a mother of a dead ten-year-old child. She addresses her son Kostas and asks him, among others, if he is not bored with sleeping in the earth and staying out at night in the black earth:[103]

Πες μας, δεν εβαρέθηκες στο χώμα να κοιμάσαι;
στη μαύρη γη να ξενυχτάς, δίχως να μας θυμάσαι; (EDT 159)
Tell us, aren't you bored of sleeping in soil?
To stay up all night without remembering us?

The last group of names of the world of the dead, or rather the phrases embodying the idea of the folk afterlife beliefs that I intend to outline here, includes the folk conviction that the Underworld is a domain of Charos, who has absolute power over the souls dwelling there. The land of Death is called correspondingly to the part of the kingdom he possesses or is actually building and, thus, makes a sort of rhetoric *pars pro toto* as, of course, it represents the whole property of Charos. The phrases describing the world below are connected with a well-known motif of the songs of Charos that we find in various versions, where he builds something, usually a palace (το παλάτι), seraglio (το σαράι), tent (η τέντα), tower (ο πύργος), or garden/orchard (το περιβόλι), using as a material the corpses of the dead of a different kind.[104]

Interestingly, the idea of a garden of Death in some demotic songs becomes altered by substituting the name of Charos by the name of the Underworld and turns into "the garden of Hades" (στου Άδη το περιβόλι, Pasayanis 1; 50). Moreover, in a song from Cyprus "the gar-

---

103 As for the motif of the personified Black Earth, see below the chapter "Charos' wedding."

104 See below the chapter "Charos the builder."

den" (το περιβόλι) is replaced by "the gardens of Charos" (στου Χάρου τους μπαξέδες, EDT 140). The same word for "garden," of Turkish origin – μπαξές (bahçe), is used in a song included by Pasayanis in his collection, with a slight but very significant and astonishing difference. The landscape of the depicted scene turns out to be the coast, the seashore, where a garden stretches with lemon trees (κει 'ναι μπαξές με λεμονιές, Pasayanis 42), and where in the middle of it one can find a cold spring into which "Go there to shave yourself, go there to change yourself" (Εκεί να πας να ξουριστείς, κι εκεί να πας ναλλάξης).

The enigmatic picture that emerges from that song at first glance is – as I suppose – a variation of the above-mentioned idea of the land of oblivion closely connected with the river of forgetfulness that is known from Ancient Greek myth, repeated subsequently and established in Roman mythology.[105] In this sense, the "change" expressed in the last verse is a symbolic passage to the other world by drinking a drop from the cold spring in the highly unusual gardens at the seashore. The land of the dead needs not be mentioned literally, it is obviously hinted at in a way that could be comprehensible and easy to guess for every listener of the cited song.

Gathering the above-mentioned names of the abode of the dead appearing in Modern Greek folk songs, we are able to see the conceptualization of afterlife beliefs according to the folk world view. The convictions concerning the place where all the souls finally go to, which emerge from the outlined attempt of linguistic categorization of the names of the other world, are plainly far from the Christian vision of heaven and hell that is a characteristic feature of folk culture in general. However, the Greek case is more specific and differs in comparison with, for instance, Slavic folk mythology. In fact, the abode of the dead according to demotic songs is echoed without any doubt in the Ancient Greek representations of the Underworld, which is confirmed not only by the names and phrases denoting it, but – more importantly – by the vision of the gloomy afterlife existence of an individual. The soul does not wander about looking for its place to rest but goes straight to the kingdom of Charos-Death, where it stays forever, longing for the upper

---

105 See, for example, Verg., Aeneid VI 705 and 713 (*Animae, quibus altera fato/ corpora debentur, Lethaei ad fluminis undam/ securos latices et longa oblivia potant*).

world that it has been ultimately deprived of, conscious of the fact that "In Hades and in Black Earth/ there are no feasts and dances" (Στον Άδη και στη Μαυρηγή/ δεν είναι γλέντια και χοροί, Pasayanis 93).

2. Charos in Modern Greek language

The vitality of the presence of the figure of Charos in Greek culture is visible not only in demotic songs, which will mainly be presented in the present book, but also in the phraseology of Modern Greek language.[106] Some fixed phrases reveal the existence of hidden mythological as well as symbolical thinking characteristic of folk culture.

Generally, as results from the comparison of some dictionaries of Modern Greek, Charos has become a usual synonym for "death" – *thanatos* (θάνατος) and a common noun to such an extent that it is written usually in small letter as χάρος, especially in more recent dictionaries.[107]

The meaning is extended into "the personification of death" (Stamatakos, Dimitrakos, Mandala, Charalambakis) or "the angel of Death" (Stamatakos) and, in one case, the dictionary gives a literary, metaphorical meaning as "fatal, death-bringing" (Dimitrakos).

Death is undoubtedly personified as Charos in the following examples and, thus, it is unjustified to write it in small letters as some dictionaries tend to. Here are some of the most typical and most commonly used phrases:

a) He appears to be a trap, difficult to avoid, an ambush, which is expressed metaphorically by the escape from some dangerous parts of Charos' body:

γλυτώνω/ξεφύγω απ' του Χάρου τα δόντια/το στόμα/τα νύχια
escape by the skin of Charos' teeth/mouth/nails

---

[106] Bzinkowski 2009: 23–24, where I enumerate some of them.

[107] Stavropoulos 1996: 965; Babiniotis 2002: 1938, who differentiate Charos as a mythological figure written with a capital letter from "charos" as a synonym for "death" (usually personified). See also: Stamatakos 1952–1955: 2895; Dimitrakos 1958: 7803; Charalambakis 2014; Mandala 2002: 1259. In this chapter I use the spelling always with a capital letter.

γλυτώνω κάποιον από τα δόντια του Χάρου
snatch somebody from the jaws of Charos

b) Charos appears to be an imminent danger, something extremely unpleasant that we are not able to get rid of or what we just hate. These phrases are used about someone we dislike and would like to avoid if possible. We could paraphrase them as: "I hate him just as I hate Charos who is going to take me":

βλέπω κάποιον σαν το Χάρο/ τον βλέπω σαν το Χάρο μου
lit. *I perceive him as Charos/ I perceive him as my Charos*

τι στέκεσαι από πάνω μου σαν το Χάρο;
lit. *Why are you standing above me like Charos?*

c) We find another interesting usage in a phrase describing someone whose life is very long, which is also very common in other languages, where we can also find a trace of folk thinking about personified death[108]:

τον ξέχασε ο Χάρος
lit. *Charos has forgotten about him*

d) Some phrases are used in reference to someone who is about to die or has just passed away:

παλεύω με το Χάρο = χαροπαλεύω
I wrestle with Charos[109]

βλέπω το Χάρο με τα μάτια μου
Look death in the face; lit. *I can see Charos through my eyes*

τον βρήκε ο Χάρος
Charos has found him

πήγε στην πόρτα του Χάρου
lit. *He went to the door of Charos*

---

[108] Eng. *Death has forgotten him*, fr. *La mort l'a oublié*, ger. *Der Tod hat ihn vergessen*, it. *La morte si è dimenticata di lui*, pol. *Śmierć o nim zapomniała*.

[109] For more on the *charopalema* motif, see the chapter "Wrestling or playing with Charos."

χτύπησε την πόρτα του Χάρου
He knocked on the door of Charos[110]

e) We find an intriguing usage of Charos in a phrase used for a person who is indifferent to the consequences of his acts that usually threaten someone's life[111]:

κι όποιον πάρει ο Χάρος!
And whoever Charos will take!

f) A phrase used jokingly during a party while raising glasses:

να πεθάνει ο Χάρος!
Let Charos die!

The trace of permeating the folk view of the world into the language might also be found in the name of a small owl that uses the name of Charos: χαροπούλι, namely "the bird of Charos."[112] According to folk beliefs, it is a bird presaging death, usually sudden and unexpected. *Charopouli* in different ethnographical accounts is an equivalent to *stringlopouli* (στριγγλοπούλι) and *klapsopouli* (κλαψοπούλι – the weeping bird).[113]

---

[110] The last two examples undoubtedly echo a biblical phrase: *the gates of Hades* (Wis 16:13). Interestingly, in Polish translations of the term, "death" appears rather instead of "Hades": *Krainy Śmierci* (Mdr 16,13), according to the translation of the Bible known as Biblia Poznańska.

[111] Interestingly, the phrase is supposed to have originated in a death game played by the Greek irregular soldiers called Armatoloi (Αρματολοί) of 1821, similar to Russian Roulette, which was strictly forbidden by the general Kolokotronis, the leader of the War of Independence in 1821. http://www.mixanitouxronou.gr/opion-pari-o-charos-pos-vgike-i-frasi-apo-ena-thanasimo-pechnidi-pou-ekane-exallo-ton-kolokotroni-emiaze-me-ti-rosiki-rouleta-ke-to-apagorefse-o-stratigos-epidi-chanontan-ilithiodos-polla-palikar/ [17.04.2017].

[112] For more on the role birds play in the eschatology of demotic songs, see my paper Bzinkowski 2012: 341. I also mentioned Charos' bird in Bzinkowski 2009: 24. I attempted to give to *χαροπούλι* the possible Latin and English equivalents identifying it as *Aegolius funereus* (Tengmalm's Owl) or, according to Lawson as *Strix aluco* (tawny owl). Lawson 1910: 312. They both belong to the owl family *Strigidae* which encompasses a lot of owls that in folk culture are associated with death.

[113] Psychogiou 2008: 307; 322; 363.

3. Charos' general characteristics

Verbs and verbal phrases

In Greek demotic songs the preference for verb and noun over adjectives is clearly visible and is a characteristic feature of demotic poetry as a whole. In that sense, Greek folk songs are more narrative than descriptive, they prefer action, movement and specifics rather that descriptions of the beauties of nature or a detailed characterisation of an object.

Thus, Charos' main characteristics could be best described by verbs or verbal phrases, which are used in relation to his person. Generally, I divided them into some groups following the common conceptual areas. For obvious reasons, I was not able to enumerate all of them, as in many cases they appear incidentally and only once.[114]

1) to take – παίρνω

The verb used most frequently regarding Charos' activities. Interestingly, we come across it in one of the oldest manuscripts containing Greek demotic songs, the above-mentioned sixteenth-century collection discovered by Sathas. The fragment seems to be rather gnomic, similarly to the other passages from that manuscript. It would be risky to decide definitely that it is the modern Greek Charos it alludes to. Yet it is worth mentioning, because it contains the expression that will become one of the most frequently used in reference to Charos in demotic songs:

> Ω χρόνοι και κακοί καιροί, αφήτε με να ζήσω,
> ή να κερδίσω τα ποθώ, ή **να με πάρη** ο Χάρος. (Pernot 1931: v. 512–513, no. 96, p. 64)[115]

---

[114] Such rare examples are "playing dice": παίζει κι ο Χάρος μια ζαριά, κείνο το νιο να πάρει. (Motsios 295 B': 274); "paint the heart": γιατί ' χω μαύρη την καρδιά, βαμμένη με μπογιάδες./ Ο Χάρος μου την έβαψε, και μπλιο τζη δεν ξεβάφει. (Detorakis 163: 170). In some cases, we also come across the rare motif of Charos singing: Ο Χάρος έκατσε ψηλά και τραγουδεί πανώρια. Anagnostopoulos 1984: 81.

[115] It is noteworthy that in Pernot's selection from Busbecq's manuscript there are no traces of Charos known from modern versions. Another example he gives is also gnomic: γιατί γυρίζω ελεύθερος και θε να με σκλαβώσης/ κ' έχω καλλιά συζώντανον του Χάρου να με δώσης. (*I walk free and you want to make me a slave/ I would prefer*

Oh years and bad times, let me live,
or I will acquire what I yearn, or let Death take me.

The following examples reveal different usage of the verb παίρνω according to the object of an action. The cited examples illustrate Charos' most typical characteristics as someone violent, resolute and unshakable. It is used mostly:

a) to define someone taken or about to be taken by Charos;

This activity is in some cases regarded as the most significant feature of Charos, the one without which he could not be called by his name, as it is explicitly expressed in a dialogue with his mother, Charissa[116]:

Όταν δεν **παίρνω** παίδαινες τσ' όταν δεν παίρνω παίδκιους,
δεν **παίρνω** τα μωρά παιδκιά, να κλαίνε οι μαννάδες
πως θα με κράζουν Χάροντα, Χάροντα πικραμμένο; (Saunier 10, 20, p. 412)
When I don't take girls and I don't take boys,
I don't take small children to make mothers cry,
How would they call me Charos, Charos the bitter?

Generally, this rapid activity is related to the prematurely dead, children and young people:

παίρν' απ' τις μάνες τα παιδιά, των αδερφιών τ' αδέρφια. (Kougeas 75; see also Kougeas 59)
He takes children from their mothers, sisters from their brothers.

---

you to give me alive to Charos/Death, Pernot v. 646–647, no. 118, Ριμάδα κόρης και νιού: 76). Characteristically, the name of Charos is always translated by Pernot as Charon, in accordance with the tendency of West Europeans. There is another fragment in Pernot's collection that attests to the usage of the verb παίρνω in the same context, however, instead of Charos an angel appears. The passage is also gnomic, because here we have the young boy talking to a girl who uses a somehow exaggerated comparison: εσύ κρατείς στα χέρια σου το πνεύμα στης ζωής μου/ κ' είσαι άγγελος με το σπαθί να πάρης την ψυχήν μου (*You keep in your hands the spirit of my life/ and you are an angel with a sword to take my life*, v. 638–639). For angelic imagery, see the chapter below: Charos and the Angels. In Pernot's anthology we also find a passage in which it is θάνατος that is not personified: να μέχε πάρη ο θάνατος την ώραν οπού σε ειδα (*I wish death took me the hour I saw it*, v. 439–440, no. 77, p. 56).

[116] See the chapter "Charos' family."

However, there are some exceptions where Charos is not independent, but it is God's will that allows or orders him to take someone[117]:

Και ο Χάρος όταν βουληθεί και ο Θεός θελήσει,
παίρνει τους νιους ξαρματογούς, τες νιες ξεστολισμένες. (Kougeas 119)
Charos, when he wants and God wants,
he takes the young boys unarmed, the young girls without ornaments.

Τη ζήλεψε ο Χάροντας και πάει για **να την πάρει.** (Motsios 50, 51, p. 179)
Charos was jealous of her and he went to take her.

Ο Χάρος μου **την πήρενε**, δεν είναι πλιο δική μου. (Motsios 281, p. 255)
Charos took her, she is no longer mine.

Που πήρενε το γιούκα τσης τον καλοπαντρεμένο. (Motsios 287, p. 261)
Who took her son, the one, who was well-married.

Occasionally, this verb appears in the words of someone who is afraid of being taken by Charos:

Κρύψε με μάνα, κρύψε με **να μη με πάρει** ο Χάρος. (Saunier 18α, p. 52. Similarly: 18β, 18γ)
Hide me, my mother, hide me, so that Charos would not take me.

There are some exceptions where death is expected to be better than an orphanage:

Πεντάρφανον εγίνηκα κ' εν έξερα χαπάρι
τώρα περικαλώ κ' εγώ το Χάρο **να με πάρει**. (Saunier 17a, p. 94; Gneutos VI)
I became a complete orphan and I knew only that,
now I beg Charos to take me.

b) in connection with the soul (ψυχή) of someone who is about to die[118];

κάνε τα χέρια σου σταυρό **να πάρω** την ψυχή σου. (EDT 129)
Make the sign of the cross so that I take your soul.

Λεβέντη μ' έστειλε ο Θεός **να πάρω** την ψυχή σου. (EDT 130, Kapsalis 628)
Young boy, God has sent me to take your soul.

---

[117] Saunier 1979: 333–339. Saunier 1999: 361; Kosegian 2010: 261–262.

[118] In some cases, Charos "takes out" (βγάζει) someone's soul, although we come across it rather rarely: καιʼ εν έπεψα σε, Χάροντα, παλκώματα να κάμης/ Παρʼ έστεκα σε, Χάροντα ψυχές για να μου βγάλλης. Cited by Omatos 1990: 311 from a Cyprian folk-song.

Χάρε που παίρνεις τις ψυχές, πάρε και τη δική μου. (Paktitis 18, p. 173)
Charos, you, who take the souls, take also my own.

c) in connection with the body (κορμί) of someone who is about to die;

Such examples differentiating the soul and the body are extremely rare:

του **παίρνει** ο Χάρος την ψυχήν και η βαρκούλα το κορμί. (Kougeas 7)
Charos takes his soul and the boat his body.

για ιδέ κορμιά που **πήρα.** (Saunier 15β, p. 404)
Have a look at the bodies I took.

d) in relation to life itself (ζωή);

Χάρε που παίρνεις τις ζωές, πάρε και τη δική μου. (Koridis 13; Paktitis 8, p. 171)
Charos, you, who take life, take also my own.

e) in relation to someone's youth (νιάτα);

μόνο με πέμπει ο Θεός τα νιάτα σου **να πάρω.** (Detorakis 155 Β', p. 167)
Only God sends me to take his youth.

f) taking by Charos as a salutary act;

According to the folk world view, death – personified by Charos – is regarded in some cases as a sort of salvation from hardship and pain. As a consequence, Charos' terrifying activity turns out to be salutary in that case.[119] This conviction manifests itself in different forms of speech, often by use of the verb παίρνω in the imperative form:

Πάρε με, Χάρε, πάρε με, **πάρε με** με τη βία
να λείψ' από τα βάσανα τσ' από την τυραννία.[120]

---

[119] Bzinkowski 2011a: 447–448. In some cases, Charos is explicitly suggested to give "mercy" (ελεημοσύνη): Παρηγοριά έχει ο θάνατος κι ελεημοσύνη ο Χάρος (Kondomichis 35).

[120] Cited by Anagnostopoulos 1984: 60. There are some cases when death is regarded as "a rest in the garden of Charos" (ανάπαψη στου Χάρου το περβόλι). We also come across a conviction that it is sometimes better to be taken by Charos than to die in a foreign land, because "Charos takes and gives relief, but a foreign land makes you feel sullen" (Ο Χάρος παίρνει και ξεγνοιάζ', η ξενιτιά μαυρίζει), Anagnostopoulos 1984: 60.

Take me, Charos, take me, take me by force
so that my torments and tortures could cease.

g) in relation to the keys (κλειδιά) that Charos took from someone;

These might be the keys to go out of Hades but as well the keys to Paradise[121]:

Μου **πήρε** ο Χάρος τα κλειδιά και πάει στην πόλη χαρωπά. (Kondomichis 47)
Charos took the keys from me and is happy going to town.

Μου **πήρε** ο Χάρος τα κλειδιά και τάβαλε στην τσέπη. (Kondomichis 8)
Charos took the keys from me and put them into the pocket.

h) in relation to the hair;

Και τα σγουρά μου τα μαλλιά ο Χάρος τα'χει πάρει. (Tsouderos 44 A', B')
And my curly hair was taken by Charos.

2) to catch, to seize, to carry off – αρπάζω, πιάνω/ put in chains – βάζω στα σίδερα

The verb αρπάζω underlining the more violent activity of Charos is often used together with the verb παίρνω:

μένα ο Χάρος μ' άρπαξε, ο <Χάροντας> με πήρε. (Saunier 13η, p. 456)
Charos caught me, Charondas took me.

Με απονιά σε άρπαξε ο έρημος ο Χάρος. (Motsios 333, p. 303)
A lonely Charos took you without compassion.

Ο Χάροντας εβιάστηκε γρήγορα να σ' αρπάξει. (Motsios 355, p. 317)
Charondas was in a hurry to seize you.

πιάνω κωπέλλιες όμορφες, άντρες πολεμιστάδες
και πιάνω και μικρά παιδιά μαζί με τους μανάδες. (EDT 129)
I catch beautiful girls, men warriors
and I catch small children together with their mothers.

---

[121] In the Kougeas collection we find a motif of stealing Charos' keys to get out from Hades: Κλέφτουν του Χάρου τα κλειδιά, του Χάρου τ' αντικλείδια (Kougeas 11). In some cases, someone begs Charos to lend him "the keys to Paradise": να μου δανείσει τα κλειδιά, κλειδιά του Παραδείσου (Saunier 12δ, p. 170).

Emphatically, this activity may be expressed by the verbal phrase "put in chains" (βάζω/ δένω στα σίδερα):

στα σίδερα τον έδεσε και στα δεσμά τον βάνει,
του βάνει και στον κόρφο του μαύρου φιδιού κεφάλι. (Ioannou 315, p. 432; Pasayanis 37)
He put him in chains, he bound him,
he put a black snake's head onto his breast.

3) to divide – χωρίζω/ to make someone an orphan – ορφανώνω

Another characteristic feature among Charos' activities reveals itself in the verbs χωρίζω and ορφανώνω, which underline the aspect of the lost connection between the dead and their relatives, rather than the separation of the soul and the body.[122] The latter happens in folk songs by use of the verb παίρνω, without any differentiation in verb as for the significance of those two components, namely the prevalence of one element above the other one.

The aspect of dividing is expressed in most cases by the verb χωρίζω in relation to mothers and children, brothers and sisters or newly-weds. This aspect of Charos' activity is expressed in two ways:

a) by Charos himself boasting about his deeds:

Για ιδέ σπίθιαν τα ρήμαξα κι αυλές αράχνιασά τσι
κι αδέρφια που ξεχώρισα, που 'σαν αγαπημένα,
κι οι στράτες καμάρωναν τα κι ο κόσμος έτρεμέν τα.
Χώρισα μάνες 'πο τα παιδιά, παιδιά 'που τσι μανάδες,
Εχώρισα κι αντρόγυνα, που 'σαν αγαπημένα.[123] (See also Saunier 15α, p. 404)
Look at the houses I destroyed and covered with cobwebs
brothers and sisters I divided, who loved each other,
the roads admired and all the people trembled with fear seeing that.
I divided mothers from children, children from mothers,
I divided couples, who loved each other so much.

[122] As for the relation of soul and body, see especially Dawkins 1942: 131–147.

[123] Cited by Anagnostopoulos 1984: 78. See Politis 213 (Το τραγούδι του Χάρου).

b) by the living who lament over the cruelty of Charos who is deaf to their pleadings[124]:

παίρνει μανάδων να παιδιά, των αδερφών τ' αδέρφια,
χωρίζει και τ' αντρόγυνα τα πολυαγαπημένα. (Saunier 6α, p. 384)
He takes children from their mothers, sisters from their brothers,
he divides couples, who love each other so much.

κάνει μανούλες δίχως γιους, γυναίκες δίχως άντρες
χωρίζει και τις αδερφές από τους αδερφούς τους. (Saunier 8δ, p. 390)
He deprives mothers of children, women of their husbands
he divides sisters from their brothers.

χωρίζεις μάνες 'που παιδιά και τα παιδιά 'π' τις μάνες
χωρίζεις τις καλόπαντρες 'που τους καλούς τους άντρες. (Saunier 13α, p. 400)
You divide mothers from children, children from brothers
you divide well-married from their good husbands.

Similarly, the verb ορφανώνω underlines the division of children and their parents:

Χάρο δεν εβαρέθηκες... να ορφανώσεις τα παιδιά; (Saunier 13γ, p. 400)
Charos, weren't you fed up with... making children orphans?

4) to destroy – διαγουμίζω (λεηλατώ), ρημάζω, διαλύω (καταστρέφω), αραχνιάζω, μαραίνω, κουρσεύω

One of the most frequent features of Charos in demotic songs manifests itself in the verbs underlining the destructive aspect of his activities. The same semantic field contains all the verbs expressing Charos' ability to "decompose" everything, break to pieces. He appears to destroy not only the relations between people by dividing the dead from the living. Metaphorically, his damaging power is extended to ruining the houses that become cobwebbed – the image often used in connection with the graves and the Underworld, which I have already mentioned above. Moreover, he is the one that makes everything wither and fade:

124 There are some examples, although quite rare, that instead of Charos, the living address their rhetorical questions, which are full of regret, towards heaven: Ω ουρανέ, που 'σαι ψηλά, κι όλον τον κόσμ' ορίζεις,/ τη μάνα απ' τα παιδάκια της, γιατί τ' αποχωρίζεις;/ Ω ουρανέ, που' σαι ψηλά, κατέβα κάμε κρίση,/ Ενού χρονού αντρόγυνο, γιατί να το χωρίσεις; cited by Anagnostopoulos 1984: 42–43. See Bzinkowski 2011a: 445.

πριν να 'ρθ ο Χάρος να μας βρει να μάσε διαγουμίσει
να διαγουμίσει τσι γεννές και να διαλέξει τς' άντρες. (Saunier 8α, p. 388)
Before Charos comes to find us and to plunder us
to plunder the generations and to choose the men.

Για ιδέ σπίθιαν τα ρήμαξα κι' αυλές αράχνιασά τση. (Saunier 15α, p. 404)
Look at the houses I destroyed and covered with cobwebs.

Χάρο δεν εβαρέθηκες... τον κόσμο να ρημάσεις; (Saunier 13γ, p. 400)
Charos, weren't you fed up with... destroying people?

ο Χάρος έρχεται και θα μας διαλύσει. (Motsios 198, p. 224)
Charos is coming to destroy us.

όλο τσι νύχτες περβατεί, όλο τσ' αυγές κουρσεύει. (Saunier 8γ, p. 388)
He constantly walks at night, he constantly pillages at dawn.

και να 'χ' ν τον αμάραντο να μην τ'ς μαραίν' ο Χάρος. (Motsios 254, p. 242)
Ah, if I had the everlasting flower so that Charos could not make it wither.

5) to kill (by an arrow, a knife, a sword) – σκοτώνω, σαϊτεύω, μαχαιρώνω, σφάζω, χτυπώ, βαρώ, έρχομαι με μαχαίρι, καίω, φαρμακώνω

Another group of verbs and verbal phrases semantically encompasses everything related to Charos' image as a merciless killer using different ways, tools and weapons to deprive someone of his life. Thus, he is sometimes called explicitly a "killer" (φονιάς), which I shall show below in the group of nouns and adjectives, he is the one who not only just "kills" (σκοτώνει) but "yearns for killing" (θέλει σκότωμα) or even "slaughters" (σφάζω):

Επερπατούσαν δυο πουλιά πάντοτε ενωμένα
κι απέρασε ο Χάροντας κι εσκότωσε το ένα. (Kapsalis 632)
Two birds walked always together
Charos passed and killed one of them.

Ο Χάρος θέλει σκότωμα με ασημένιες μπάλες. (Kapsalis 622; Paktitis 2, p. 170; see also Motsios 355, p. 317; Motsios 319, p. 289)
Charos wants killing with silver bullets.

Σφάζει παιδιά, αντί για αρνιά, γυναίκες για προβάτες,
σφάζει πρωτοπαλίκαρα αντί παχιά κριάρια. (Koridis 23)
He slaughters children, instead of lambs,
he slaughters the bravest young instead of fat rams.

Among the weapons he uses, significantly, the most common are a knife (μαχαίρι, μαχαιρώνω), a bow and arrows (σαϊτεύω) or he just hits (βαρώ, χτυπώ)[125]:

Χάρε, και τι σου κάναμε, κι όλο μας μαχαιρώνεις. (Motsios 348, p. 313; see also Ioannou 276, p. 391)
Charos, what have we done to you so that all the time you knife us?

και πάει την εμαχαίρωσε, ταχιά μέσα στο σπίτι. (Kapsalis 649)
And he went and knifed her, quickly in the house.

κι ο Χάρος ήρτε δίπλα μου με δίκοπο μαχαίρι. (Motsios 346, p. 311)
Charos came closer to me with a doubled-edged knife.

του Χάρου το μαχαίρι/ που πήρε τη γυναίκα μου. (Saunier 9, p. 84)
The knife of Charos/ that took my wife.

γυιέ μου που σ'ηύρ' ο χάροντας κι εμαχαιρόσφαξέ σε. (Kriaris, pp. 201–202)
My son, whom Charos found and slaughtered with a knife.

ο Χάροντας επέρασε και εσαΐεψέ μας. (Motsios 296, p. 276)
Charondas passed by and killed us with arrows.

τσ' εβγήκε τσ' εσαΐτεψε την μονασήν την κόρην. (Saunier 19β, p. 410)
He came out and shot by arrow our only daughter.

κι ο Χάρος τη σαΐτεψε μες το δεξί το χέρι. (Sklavenitis 2, p. 48)
And Charos shot her by arrow into her right hand.

ο Χάρος την εχτύπησε σε μια τοποθεσία. (Motsios 350, p. 315)
Charos hit her in some place.

Βαρεί τις μάνες στην καρδιά, τις αδερφές στα σκώτια,
τις χήρες τις κακόμοιρες μέσα στα φυλλοκάρδια. (Ioannou 281, p. 396)
He shoots mothers in the heart, sisters in the livers,
the miserable widows in the bottom of their hearts.

Other interesting verbs used in the same context and belonging to the same semantic field are καίω (to burn) and φαρμακώνω (to poison):

θέλω να καίω αδερφές, να λαχταρίζω μάνες. (Ioannou 277, p. 392)
I want to burn sisters, to make mothers miss.

---

[125] Alexiou 1978: 227; Anagnostopoulos 1984: 74f. we also find a sword (το σπαθί) and a spear (το κοντάρι). In some very rare cases, Charos also uses a West European attribute of Death, "a sickle" or "a scythe" (το δρεπάνι). See the chapter "Charos the Reaper."

Ανάθεμα το χάροντα, που ήρθε να με κάψει.
να πάρει τη μανούλα μου, στα μαύρα να με βάψει. (Paktitis 5, p. 170)
Curse on Charos, who came to burn me.
to take my beloved mother, to paint me in black.

'πως μ'έκαψεν ο Χάροντας, δε μ'έκαψ' άλλο πράμα. (Tsouderos 13)
The way Charos burnt me, no other thing burnt me.

Ο Χάρος εκατέβηκε μ' ένα χρυσό ποτήρι
φαρμάκωσε τον άντρα μου, τον πρώτο νοικοκύρη. (Paktitis 15, p. 172)
Charos descended with a golden cup
he poisoned my husband, the first host.

6) to call, to invite – καλώ/ to receive – δέχομαι

There are also some verbs used in relation to Charos' activities that definitely have no negative explicit connotations as the other ones cited above. They circle around the idea of Charos as a host of the Underworld that "invites" (καλεί) to his son's wedding:[126]

ο Χάρος τον εκάλεσε, παντρεύει τον υγιό του. (Pasayannis 93)
Charos invited him, he marries his son.

Surprisingly, I have also found an example where a young girl confesses that she had been called by Charos so that he could kiss her, in other words, to greet her in the world below:

με κάλεσεν ο Χάροντας να πάω να με φιλέψει. (Motsios 75, p. 186)
Charos has called me to kiss me.

Ξύπνα και πες μου, μάτια μου, το πώς σε δέχτη ο Χάρος; (Pasayanis 47, p. 25)
Wake up and tell me, my beloved, how Charos received you?

Να το ήξερα παιδάκι μου, το πώς σε δέχτη ο Χάρος,
εάν σε δέχτηκε καλά, λαμπάδα να του στείλω. (Ioannou 296, p. 411; see also 297, 298, Matsinopoulos E-11)
I wish I knew, my child, how Charos received you,
if he received you well, so that I could send him a torch.

7) to be jealous, to envy – ζηλεύω

Μ' εζήλεψε μας τη φωλιά ο έρημος ο Χάρος. (Motsios 329, p. 299)
The lonely Charos was jealous about our nest.

---

[126] See the chapter "Charos' wedding."

τη ζήλεψε ο Χάροντας και πάει να την πάρει. (Kapsalis 654)
Charos was jealous about her and he came to take her.

8) to deceive – πλανώ, γελώ

One of the most typical characteristics of Charos is his predilection for deceiving people.[127] According to the folk world view, death appears to be a deceiver who takes people using different tricks, who sets unavoidable traps[128]:

Ο Χάρος μας επλάνεσε και δεν μπορώ να φύγω. (Saunier 14α, p. 402)
Charos deceived us and I cannot escape.

Όμορφα που με γέλασεν ο Χάρος να με πάρει. (Saunier 14β, p. 402)
How cunningly Charos deceived me to take me.

Μη σε γελάσει ο Χάροντας και μη σε ξεπλανέσει. (Saunier 4θ, p. 266)
Let Charos not deceive you, let him not delude you.

Μα ξαφνικά και πρόωρα σε γέλασε ο Χάρος. (Motsios 328, p. 298)
But abruptly and prematurely Charos deluded you.

Ήρθεν ο Χάρος κι ηύρε σε και περιπλάνησε σε. (Motsios 348, p. 313)
Charos came and found you and deluded you.

Nouns and adjectives

Most of Charos' influence on people could be described by the word "wrongdoer" (αδικητής, παραδικητής) which indicates that he is supposed to commit something bad or illegal.[129] Closely connected with this epithet, and the semantic field it sends back, are the nouns emphasizing Charos as an enemy, according to the folk view of the world. Thus, he is also regarded as a killer (φονιάς), a pirate (κουρσάρος), a thief (κλέφτης) or "the first thief" (πρωτοκλέφτης), who uses tricks and sets up ambushes to steal a man's life or the keys to Paradise/Hades.[130] This

[127] Saunier 1979: 319.

[128] There is one interesting example that we find only in Laconia in Mani, where Charos gathers people on the rock and sneers at them (τους κογιονάρει): Ο Χάρος τους εμάζωξε σε μια καημένη ράχη/ κι απόντες τους εμάζωξε, πιάνει τους κογιονάρει (Pasayanis 2, p. 13; 22, pp. 18–19; Saunier 16, p. 404; Ioannou 285, p. 400).

[129] Saunier 1979: 317–323.

[130] Anagnostopoulos 1984: 78 ff.

activity, so strongly connected with the belief that Charos-Death may appear unexpectedly and that it is impossible to flee from him, is met in other names folk imagination gave him. Most commonly he is called a hunter (κυνηγητής) and a peddler (πραματευτής).[131] The following examples clearly show that sometimes these nouns may occur together and Charos can be called both a hunter and a pirate in one song. This fact indicates the formulaic character of noun qualifiers that may be replaced by one another and are not necessarily meaningful. The repetition of the first hemistich so that the second one may seem different and that the narrative could evolve is a characteristic feature of demotic poetry.[132] Here are some examples:

> Καλότυχα είναι τα βουνά, καλότυχοί ειν' οι κάμποι,
> που Χάρο δεν εκαρτερούν, φονιά δεν περιμένουν. (Saunier 6, 336; Ioannou 280, p. 395; Politis 211)
> *The mountains are happy, the fields are lucky,*
> *that they don't wait for Charos, they don't await the killer.*
>
> Ο Χάρος είν' αδικητής, είναι κρυφός κουρσάρος
> όλο τσι νύχτες περβατεί, όλο τσ' αυγές κουρσεύει. (Saunier 8γ, p. 388)
> *Charos is a criminal, he is a hidden pirate*
> *he constantly walks at night, he constantly pillages at dawn.*
>
> Ο Χάρος είναι πονηρός, 'πιτήδιος πρωτοκλέφτης,
> ξέρει κλεφτοπατήματα, πονήριες γυναικώνε.[133]
> *Charos was a cunning and skilful first thief,*
> *he knows a thief's steps, women's artifices.*
>
> γιατ' έχω γιον πραματευτήν τσαι γιον πρωτοκουρσάρον. (EDT 141; Pasayanis 33, p. 21)
> *Because I have a son the peddler, a son the first pirate.*
>
> γιάτι έχω γιο κυνηγητή, γιατί έχω γιο κουρσάρο. (Kapsalis 651; Sklavenitis 15, p. 58)
> *Because I have a son the hunter, a son the pirate.*
>
> Ω Χάρε παραδικητή, παραδικιές που κάμνεις. (Saunier, 13α, p. 400; Gneutos VIII)
> *Charos, you criminal, the crimes you commit.*

---

131 For a more detailed analysis of the qualifiers concerning Charos as a hunter and a peddler, see the next chapter.

132 Kosegian 2010: 39–40.

133 Cited by Anagnostopoulos 1984: 58, 78.

Ο Χάρος είναι γελαντζής και είν' και πολύ μαριόλος,
σαν κλέφτης μπάνει στο χωριό και σαν κουρσάρος βγαίνει. (Saunier 8δ, p. 390)
Charos is a deceiver and very cunning,
he enters like a thief into the village, like a pirate he goes out.

The adjectives that generally appear rather rarely, which I have already mentioned, tend to emphasize Charos as "deceptive" (επίβουλος), "merciless" and "heartless" (άσπλαχνος, άπονος), "bitter" (πικρός)[134] and "greedy" (αχόρταγος).[135] On rare occasions, he is also called "mindless" (ασυλλόγιστος)[136]:

Χάρε γιατ' είσαι άσπλαχνος, Χάρε για δε λυπάσαι; (Saunier 13δ, p. 402)
Charos, why are you merciless, Charos, why don't you pity?

Ο Χάρος είναι άπονος, καθόλου δεν λυπάται. (Motsios 352, p. 316)
Charos has no compassion, he does not pity at all.

Χάρε πικρέ αχόρταγε, ανήμερο θηρίο. (Paktitis 21, p. 173)
Charos, bitter and greedy, an untameable beast.

Χάροντα, πικροχάροντα κι όχεντρας κληρονόμε
μ' άναψες τέτοια πυρκαγιά που σβήσιμο δεν παίρνει. (Sklavenitis 10, p. 5)
Charondas, bitter Charondas and heir of the viper
you lighted such a big fire that it is not possible to extinguish.

Χάρε μου ασυλλόγιστε, συλλογισμό δεν έχεις
κ' ήρθες και μας αδίκησες απότου δα που στέκεις. (Saunier 13β, p. 400)
Charos, you mindless, you unmindful
you came and you did injustice to us right there where you stand.

Interestingly, in some specific cases, Charos is not equipped only with threatening features, he gains an almost human appearance and looks tired, like in the following example that probably is exclusively Cretan, where he is described as "pale" (χλωμός) and "withered" (μαραμένος, Saunier 17, p. 406; Ioannou 283, p. 398 [Kriaris 228]) However, such an appearance may also be caused by the slaughter he had just made and then the picture would be rather ironic and sullen than "human."[137]

[134] One of the common names of Charos is Πικροχάροντας or – as a metathesis – Πρικοχάροντας. In a song from Lefkada this feature of Charos is multiplied: Χάροντα, Πικροχάροντα, και Βαρυπικραμένε. (Kondomichis 4). For other interesting epithets of Charos, see especially Anagnostopoulos 1984: 86.

[135] Anagnostopoulos 1984: 78.

[136] Saunier 1979: 319.

[137] Anagnostopoulos 1984: 76.

Sometimes he is even called "alone" (έρημος), which underlines his loneliness in executing his duties as a personification of death[138]:

μόν' σκιάζομαι το θάνατο, τον έρημο το Χάρο. (Kapsalis 629)
I only tremble with the fear of death, the lonely Charos.

ο έρημος ο Χάρος, λεβέντη μου
άνοιξη σε θέρισε. (Kapsalis 658)
The lonely Charos, my boy
he reaped you in spring.

Some specific adjectives are also used to describe the appearance of Charos, however, besides the most common of them, "black" (μαύρος)[139], which is used very often, they appear extremely rarely and rather in nineteenth-century collections of demotic songs.[140] According to some of them, Charos is sometimes depicted as "barefooted" (ξυπόλητος, ξεσκάλτσωτος), dressed in shining clothes (λαμπροφρεμένος) – which is striking because usually he is completely black – with eyes like lightning (της αστραπής τα μάτια, σαν αστραπή 'ν' το βλέμμα του).[141]

---

[138] Obviously, these examples don't exhaust all the possible options as for the usage of adjectives. For instance, only in Cyprus do we come across the representation of Charos as a blind man (στραόν μ' έναν αμμάτι). We come across the adjective used in the Cypriot version for "blindness" (στραβός) in some representations of Charos as lame. Yet, they are not common in demotic songs, but we come across them rather in folk stories. Two fragments from the Mani Peninsula are also interesting, where Charos is depicted as "ruthless," "hard" (σκληροχάρος) and another one, where apparently this adjective has been distorted and a new phrase has been coined from it, basing on structural similarity: σκληρός-σκύλος. Here Charos is called "Charos the dog" (σκυλοχάρος): και απέκει του μετάνωσε του Χάρου σκυλοχάρου (Kougeas 3: 39), Μα ο Χάρος ο σκληρόχαρος τα κεραμίδια βγάνει (Kougeas 59).

[139] See the next chapter: "Hunter, Horseman, Black Rider," where I allude several times to the motif of Charos' black colour.

[140] Most of them are cited by Anagnostopoulos 1984: 74–75 mainly from Politis, *Akritika*... 10; 47; Passow 304; 430; Lambrakis 61.

[141] In two examples cited by Anagnostopoulos we find a very interesting and rare representation of Charos as "dressed in lynx fur" (πώχει του ρίτσου τα πλουμιά). Anagnostopoulos 1984: 74.

4. Charos' specific characteristics

Hunter, Horseman, Black Rider[142]

In a well-known, at least to Greek readers, poem by Kostis Palamas, *Digenis and Charos* (*Ο Διγενής κι ο Χάροντας*), Death, obviously personified here as Charos, takes Digenis to Hades on his horse (Καβάλα πάει ο Χάροντας/ το Διγενή στον Άδη). It seems that this image is so deeply rooted in Greek consciousness and has become so natural that beyond all doubt it should not provoke astonishment nor inspire questions. However, as I will attempt to show, such a picture is more enigmatic and complicated than it appears and – yet more important – arouses doubts as to the possible origins of such a representation.

According to the folk world view, Charos as Death is a constant persecutor of mankind, following every step of man and casting a shadow on all human efforts. Probably such a universal – archetypal in mythic terms – conviction may constitute the basis of the image of Death as a tireless hunter. There are some examples in Greek folk songs where he appears to be a double-image of a man, a sort of his *eidolon* in behaviour, which is visible, for instance, in the following song from Pontus based on the motif of wrestling with Charos[143]:

> Χάρε, ντο έχεις μετ' εμέν και πάντ' ακολουθάς με,
> κι αν κάθουμαι, συγκάθεσαι, κι αν περπατώ, ακολουθάς με
> κι αν κείμαι ν' αποκοιμηθώ, γίνεσαι μαξιλάρι μ';[144]
> *Charos, what do you have against me that you always follow me,*
> *when I sit, you sit with me, when I walk, you follow*
> *and when I go to bed for sleep, you become my pillow?*

If we assume that Charos acts as a personification of Death in this example, the image would reveal a somehow curious eschatological dimension. Thus, Death would appear not as a sort of persecutor but rather a guardian angel, however, strikingly, in a completely different and astonishing context, metaphorically as a pillow (μαξιλάρι) to sleep for

---

[142] Some parts of the texts in this chapter are loosely based on my conference paper: Bzinkowski, Serrano 2015.

[143] Bzinkowski 2011a: 447.

[144] Cited by Anagnostopoulos 1984: 47.

ever on. This is obviously the mechanism of euphemism, well-known to folk thinking and its tendency to substitute in a language the things that appear to be unpleasant or offensive by milder ones.

In fact, the above-mentioned example is just an elaboration of an idea of Charos as a hunter unceasing in his practice of tracking down his prey, the image obviously weakened here by the mention of "a pillow" that makes the horror of hunting by Death more tolerable.

The figure of Charos as a huntsman in Modern Greek folk songs is inextricably mingled with his representations as a black horse rider and it is very difficult to present and analyse them separately.

Significantly, it is Charos' mother, Charissa or Charondissa,[145] who sometimes describes him as an unceasing hunter. She addresses other mothers to hide their children from him. We come across interesting examples in Kougeas' collection of Maniatic songs. Charondissa warns the other ones about her son and orders them to shut the door and gather the children:

γιατί βγήκε ο υιός μου αποβραδίς να πολυκυνηγήσει
Δεν κυνηγάει πέρδικες, δεν κυνηγά ελάφια,
κυνηγά των μάνων τα παιδιά, των γυναικών τους άντρες. (Kougeas 22 α')
Because my son at dusk goes hunting
He does not hunt for partridges, does not hunt for deer;
Only he hunts for mothers' children, women's husbands.

γιατί είν' ο γιος μου κυνηγός και κυνηγάει τες ρούγες. (Kougeas 127)
Because my son is a hunter and he hunts in the neighbourhood.

γιατ' έχω γιο κυνηγητή. (Sklavenitis 15, p. 58)
Because I have a son the hunter.

The same motif is found in a song from North Epirus, but here it is someone saying that he supposedly heard Charos' mother shouting so that women hide their husbands, sisters their brothers, young girls their beloved ones, and mothers their children:

τι ο γιος μου βγήκε παγανιά, εβγήκε για κυνήγι,
δεν κυνηγά στις ερημιές, δεν κυνηγά στους κάμπους,
διαλέγει το κυνήγι του κι όπου αρέσει παίρνει. (Kapsalis 640, 652)
Because my son went on a hunt, went on a chase,

145 See the chapter "Charos' family."

he does not hunt in the deserted places nor in the fields,
he chooses his prey and he takes it wherever he likes.

In another version, Charos sets out for a real hunting trip, trying to shoot some animals, however, he does not succeed and heads for human prey:

Βγήκε ο Χάρος παγανιά να λαφοκυνηγήσει [...]. (Ioannou 281, p. 396; Saunier 5β, p. 282)
Charos went hunting for deer [...].

Βαρεί τις μάνες στην καρδιά, τις αδερφές στα σκώτια,
τις χήρες τις κακόμοιρες, μέσα στα φυλλοκάρδια. (Ioannou 281, p. 396, Pramanta, Epirus)
He shoots mothers in the heart, sisters in the livers,
the miserable widows in the bottom of their hearts.

We also come across exactly the same formula (βγήκε...) in a song from Leukada in Saunier's collection, although in a different context. Here we deal rather with a motif of "the procession of Charos" that I will present in another place.[146] In Saunier's collection, in a song from Propylaia, Charos is called by his mother κυνηγός, who does not hunt for deer (δεν κυνηγάει αλάφια) but young ones and children (Saunier 6γ, p. 384).

In a different version, Charos' mother addresses herself to her son:

Γιε μ' στο κυνήγι που θα πας και στο κυνήγημά σου (Saunier 7, p. 386)[147]
My son, during the hunt you will go on, during your hunting.

In a short song from Elos in Crete, the person speaking asks Charos why he is unyielding in his activity as a hunter:

Χάροντα γιάντα κυνηγάς τον κόσμο τον καημένο; (Saunier 13γ, p. 400)
Charos, why do you hunt for miserable people?

Charos as a huntsman is in some cases represented on horseback, like in this song from Leukada, where his destroying activity is emphasized, as is the fact he acts as a conqueror:

Εβγήκε ο Χάρος παγανιά να κάψει την καρδιά μας.
Κρύψτε γυναίκες τς άντρες σας, γυναίκες τα παιδιά σας

---

[146] See the chapter "Procession of Charos."

[147] From Passow 291, 408 who used the subsequent collections: Zambelios 732, 19 and Tomasseo 293. See Saunier 1999: 387.

κι εσείς θλιμμένες αδερφές να κρύψετε τα' αδέρφια.
Μα ο Χάρος δεν στομώνεται κι η πίκρα δεν τον πιάνει.
Όταν σελλώνει τ' άλογο, τα σπίτια τα ρημάζει. (Kondomichis 5, p. 171)
My son went hunting to burn our hearts.
Women, hide your husbands, women hide your children
and you broken-hearted sisters, hide your brothers.
But Charos is implacable, bitterness does not touch him.
When he saddles his horse, he destroys the houses.

Sometimes Charos as a hunter or horseman is accompanied by his hounds (ζαγάρια). However, such examples are not so frequent as one would expect, which makes this case very interesting. The rare frequency of such an image questions this concept as a Greek one, which I shall discuss later. It is symptomatic that the above-mentioned motif of hunting does not necessarily encompass the hounds. This element appears in connection with the representation of Charos as a black horseman, which will be discussed subsequently. The mention of the hounds always follows the black rider or black horseman motive and it is not possible to separate these two elements.

βλέπω το Χάρο κι έρχεται στους κάμπους καβελάρης.
Μαύρος είναι, μαύρα φορεί, μαύρο 'ν' και τ' άλογό του,
μαύρο 'ν' το ζαγάρι του, που έρχεται κοντά του. (Petropoulos, p. 250, Γ', Αρκαδία)
I see Charos coming through the fields on a horse.
He is black, he is dressed in black, his horse is black,
his hound, following him, is black.

In a song from Mani, a version of a well-known motif "Charos and a Shepherd" (Ο Χάρος και ο τσοπάνης), Charos is requested to take his tent (τέντα), his horses and hounds and go away to the other district (ρούγα), but his answer leaves no doubt as to his intentions:

'Πάρε, Χάρε, την τέντα σου, πήγαινε σ' άλλη ρούγα.
να φάνε τ' άτια σου ταγή και τ' άλογα σου στάρι
να φαν και τα ζαγάρια σου αφράτο παξιμάδι.
Τ' άλογα θέλουν γέροντες, τ' άτια μου παλληκάρια,
θέλουν και τα ζαγάρια μου μικρών παιδιών κεφάλια.' (KEEL 333, 2, 6, Gytheio 1893, Nestoridis)[148]
'Take away, Charos, your tent, go to the other district.
So that your steeds eat some feed, your horses eat some wheat
so that your hounds eat some fluffy rusks.

[148] Cited by Saunier 1982: 302–303.

Horses want old men, my steeds want the brave young,
my hounds want small children's heads.'

The three elements mentioned here, namely Charos' tent, his horses and hounds, do not often appear together, which makes the fragment very interesting. Usually, Charos is depicted as a black-dressed horseman, always – which is worth underlining, because it is one of his unchangeable features – with a black horse (μαύρο άλογο). This representation in many different versions is undoubtedly Pan-Hellenic, we find it in every part of Greece,[149] which does not mean that it is Hellenic at all, as I shall try to elucidate below.

The main characteristics of Charos in this kind of representation is the colour black: his garments as well as his horse are invariably black[150]:

Μα να τον και κατέβαινε τσου κάμπους καβαλλάρης
μαύρος ήταν, κατάμαυρος, μαύρο και τ' άλογό του (Saunier, 6δ, p. 386, Kefalonia; see also Saunier, 8γ, p. 388, Ιθάκη; Petropoulos 82 Γ', p. 250, Β')
And here he is descending to the fields on a horse
he was black, totally black, black was his horse.

Occasionally, he also has a black scarf (μαντίλι) on his neck and head (Μαύρο μαντίλι στο λαιμό και μαύρο στο κεφάλι, Petropoulos 91 Δ', p. 254, Δ', Λευκάδα).

Undoubtedly, in the fragments cited above regarding the representation of Charos as a hunter or a black horseman, different folk notions as for the personification of death have mingled. What is striking and significant is that none of them may be traced to the Greek antiquity. There are no representations of any god belonging to the mythological cosmos of eschatological images, which are composed by use of the black horse imagery.

Any attempts made by scholars at dealing with the question – it is worth underlining, rather seldom ones – to decipher the origins of such representations so far have been in vain. In studies by Alexiou,[151] whose approach to the problem is regarded as the most complex and thorough, we do not find any solution of this representation, nor even a slightest

---

[149] Saunier 1982, 313.

[150] In very rare cases, he is depicted as dressed in shining clothes (λαμπροφορεμένος), which I have already alluded to.

[151] Alexiou 1978. Alexiou 2002.

clue that could be traced. The question was raised several times in older studies by Moravcsik and Hesseling[152] who merely suggested the possible West European sources of the representation of Charos on horseback. In more up-to-date scholarship, the issue was alluded to, among others, by Anagnostopoulos,[153] Saunier[154] and Bakker – Van Gemert[155] but so far satisfying results as for the proposed solutions have not been obtained.

According to Anagnostopoulos' suggestion, a possible source of such a representation of Charos might be an elaboration of the well-known biblical image known as The Four Horsemen of the Apocalypse (Book of Revelation 6:1–8). Such a suggestion obviously lacks a solid base due to the fact that the horseman who rides a black horse (ἵππος μέλας, 6, 5) in this passage is known as a personification of Famine (Λιμός). Death as the forth horseman, besides the only one mentioned by name, rides a pale horse (ἵππος χλωρός, 6, 8).

Anagnostopoulos also mentions that we come across such an image in Ioannis Pikatoros' from Rethymnon "Mournful Rhyme on the Bitter and Insatiable Hades" (Ρίμα θρηνητική εις τον πικρόν και ακόρεστον Άδην), written after 1519.[156] The work is a version of, popular in Byzantine and post-Byzantine literature, variations of *katabasis*,[157] however, it is very original when compared with other works belonging to this genre. The author must have drawn inspiration from very different sources,

---

152 Moravcsik 1930; Hesseling 1897, 1930, 1931.

153 Anagnostopoulos 1984: 77.

154 Saunier 1982: 302. Saunier 1972, 148.

155 Bakker – Van Gemert 2008: 5.

156 Anagnostopoulos 1984: 75–76.

157 For the most comprehensive and still up-to-date survey of the *katabasis* motif in Byzantine and post-Byzantine literature, see Lambakis 1982. Significantly, there is no personalized Charos in the second significant work of Cretan Renaissance, *Apokopos*, ascribed to Bergadis and published in Venice in 1509. Charos is mentioned three times, but is completely insignificant for the writer: διατί στον Άδην τους πετά συζώντανους ο Χάρος. (255), και ο Χάρος μας εδέχθηκεν σύμψυχους εις τον Άδην. (364), και θάνατος ο δρόμος μας και το ταξίδιν Χάρος (400). Αλεξίου, Σ.: Μπεργαδή, Απόκοπος. Η Βοσκοπούλα, Ερμής, Αθήνα 1971. According to Van Gemert, Apokopos was a reaction to the traditional image of the Underworld we find in Pikatoros' Mournful Rhyme and is purposely contrasted with it, regarding the mood and the eschatological imagery. There have been many interpretations of the poem, but generally all agree that it is not a moralizing work. Van Gemert 1991: 65.

including other literary works, Greek folk tradition as well as paintings. In his *katabasis* he made Charos/Death himself the guide of the Underworld, who – riding a black horse – shows the torments of Hades to the protagonist of the story.[158] The description abounds with elements from West European apocalypses or *katabasis* stories, such as dragon-death, river of the dead, a bridge of trials, the guardian of Hades, and Death as a killer.[159] The description of Charos-guide appears to be similar to the cited above fragments of folk songs, although his appearance is more threatening:

Κι είδα τον Χάρο κι έμπαινε κι έβγαινε θυμωμένος,
σαν μακελάρης και φονιάς τα χέρια ματωμένος,·
μαύρον εκαβαλίκευε, εβάστα και κοντάρι
κι εκράτειεν εις την χέραν του σαγίτα και δοξάρι
κι είχε θωριάν αγριόθωρη, μαύρη κι αλλοτριομένη
κι η φορεσιά του χάλκινη και καταματωμένη. (66–71)
And I saw Charos, who was going to and fro angrily,
as a butcher or a killer with his bloodstained hands,
he was sitting on a black horse, kept a spear
and in the other hand had an arrow and a bow
and he was wild in appearance, black and alienated
and his garments were made of bronze and bloodstained.

Mournful Rhyme has nothing in common with the above-mentioned *Apokopos* and is overflowing with macabre images,[160] which makes it closer to West European texts belonging to medieval folk culture known as *Dialogues between Man and Death*.[161] Although we have no traces of their existence in Byzantine scholar literature, there are some examples of their usage in a few texts that were written in demotic language in the last period of Byzantium.[162] One could even have the impression that

[158] Van Gemert 1991: 65–67.

[159] Bakker – Van Gemert 2008: 44.

[160] "Mournful Rhyme" is closer to the still unpublished "Παλαιά και Νέα Διαθήκη" in 5329 lines which is a dialogue between a man and Death as well as a monologue of Charos, who is described as very friendly and has nothing in common either with West European medieval images or with the terrifying Charos from demotic songs. Panagiotakes 1995: 311–312.

[161] Hesseling 1931: 133. Panagiotakes 1995: 311–313.

[162] Three such poems are cited by Moravcsik 1931: 61–68, another two by Hesseling 1897: 56–63. See also: Knös 1962: 312; Alexiou 1978, 225–226; Omatos 1990: 306; Panagiotakes 1995: 312–313.

the author of *Mournful Rhyme* must have seen somewhere the late medieval allegorical representations from the fourteenth and fifteenth centuries known as *Danse Macabre* or *Dances of Death*, of French-German origins[163] – completely absent in Greece[164] – where Death as a skeleton forces people to dance.

Naturally, this is just a supposition devoid of any convincing proof. Moreover, Death in Pikatoros is not a skeleton but a fully armed warrior, which may exclude the possibility of such an influence.

As Alexis Politis convinces, there was constant and mutual interference between the learned tradition – in this case written – and demotic oral poetry.[165] There are known folk songs containing modified passages from *Mournful Rhyme* and the Cretan tragedy *Erofili* of Georgios Chortatsis. Consequently, we could suppose that the image of Charos riding a black horse that we come across in many demotic songs might have originated in the work of Cretan Renaissance, but also in this case the proof is rather frail and not so easy to verify.

According to Saunier,[166] such a representation of Charos as a conqueror has probably originated as a distant recollection in the collective memory of Greek society that throughout centuries was threatened by external attacks, constantly from the fifteenth until nineteenth century, especially of the pirates, which I shall discuss below. The question of the origins in the context of historical events is still open for discussion and so far no satisfying result has been achieved.[167]

Another very enticing suggestion was made at the end of the nineteenth century by Hesseling.[168] He put forward a proposal that the image of Charos on a black horse might be compared with the well-known, and widespread through the Balkans, the Aegean and even in Asia Mi-

163 Vovelle 2008: 129–132.

164 Hesseling 1931: 134. Van Gemert 1991: 67.

165 Politis A. 2011: 284–292.

166 Saunier 1982: 302–303.

167 Bakker – Van Gemert 2008: 5. There is some similarity between the representation of Charos as a black rider and black horses of *the Akrites*, but any attempt to link them both is doomed to failure due to methodological as well as textual reasons: all the texts, including most of the acritic songs, as it has been suggested several times, might have originated in the nineteenth century. Politis A. 2011: 55.

168 Hesseling 1931: 188–189.

nor, funerary relief with a motif of a hunter on horseback, known as the "Thracian horseman" or "Thracian rider." They were used as a votive relief to different deities as well as – more importantly to us – a funerary stele. The name of the relief is connected with the place it appears more often, namely in Thrace, and from 2000 such objects that have been found, some of them are Hellenistic but most originated in Roman times.[169] The scene that is depicted on the relief is very interesting for our consideration: a rider, mostly turned to the right,[170] sitting on a horse, in some types presented as a hunter or heading for hunting or just coming back from it, in some cases followed by his hound.[171]

The Thracian Rider relief, regarded as an example of religious syncretism, in which we could recognize mythological elements from Greek, Roman, Thracian and Eastern traditions, with the recognizable features of many other divinities, originated in Greek art, especially in funerary reliefs of the heroised dead.[172] Although, as it is assumed, it reflects Thracian beliefs in immortality, the figure of the hero on horseback is not easily explainable and still gives rise to many doubts. However, the eschatological context – so important for our purposes – even if it may seem at first view as incoherent and deprived of connection with the explanation of Charos as a black rider, and with Modern Greek folk culture – should definitely be taken into account, in my opinion. Moreover, as it turns out, the figure of the Thracian Rider plays an important role in another neighbouring folk tradition, the Serbian one. There, the Thracian horseman (Трачки коњаник) plays the role of an intermediary between the world of gods and this world and is regarded as a chthonic divinity.[173] These obvious similarities clearly show that the relation between the Serbian horseman and Greek Charos riding a black horse is definitely worth further investigation, taking into account the context of intercultural Balkan folk traditions, which is beyond the scope of this book.

---

169 Dimitrova 2002: 209–210.

170 This kind of representation is preserved in Christian art. Saint Demetrios and Saint Georgios are depicted exactly in this way.

171 Dimitrova 2002: 210–214, where we find the exact classification of the motives presented on the reliefs with the Thracian Horseman.

172 Dimitrova 2002: 211; 220.

173 http://www.svevlad.org.rs/bajoslovlje/petrovic_mitologija.html [23.04.2017].

Reaper

In some cases, different representations of Charos seem to have mixed up in folk imagination, creating a mosaic image of mutually excluding elements. In the following example, the figure of Charos as a hunter is surprisingly extended into the well-known archetypal picture of Death as a Reaper:

> και βγήκε ο γιός μου παγανιά και παίρνει και θερίζει. (Kondomichis 34, p. 151, Leukada)
> *And my son sets out for hunting, he takes and reaps.*

The association between life perceived as the cycle of vegetation, which all plants and living beings are subjected to, has accompanied human thinking from the beginning of mankind. In Greek antiquity, the concept of death harvesting the crop of life is well rooted and we could find many examples of such an idea in Greek literature as well as in art. In particular, the idea of flowers or fruit, prematurely cut, recurs in the most archaic fragments of lyric poetry.[174]

The parallel coexistence of man and nature, their juxtaposition as well as the comparison of a human's life to that of a plant reiterates in all Modern Greek folk poetry. In particular, *mirologia* abound in the images of spring and flowers with reference to women, in most cases the young ones.[175] Thus, the metaphor of the beauty of nature in springtime is used to stress the cruelty of Charos-Death and simultaneously to express deep regret for the loss of children prematurely taken:

> Για ιδές καιρό που διάλεξες, Χάρε μου, να τον πάρης,
> 'ς τα έβγα του καλοκαιριού, 'ς τα έμπα του χειμώνα,
> να πάρης τάνθη όχ τα βουνά, λελούδια από τους κάμπους,
> να πάρης τον αμάραντο, να τον μαράν' η πλάκα. (Politis 192)
> *Look at the season that you chose, my Charos, to take me,*
> *at the end of summer, at the beginning of winter,*
> *to take flowers from the mountains, flowers from the fields,*
> *to take the everlasting flower so that the grave makes it wither.*

---

174 Alexiou 2002b: 195. She cites a very graphic and useful example of the idea of reaping from a fragment of Eurypides: *βίον θερίζειν ὥστε κάρπιμον στάχυν* (E. Hyps. fr. 757 Nauck). See also Omatos 1990: 310–311.

175 Bzinkowski 2011a: 446.

The death of a child is sometimes compared to the gathering of unripe fruit or to still green apples shaken by the north wind:

'Τάχ' το, η μάννα μου, πως ήσουνα μηλίτσα,
άνθισες μικρή και κάρπισες μεγάλη,
φύσηξε βοριάς, σ' τα τίνιαξε τα μήλα.' (Politis 210)
'Suppose, my mother, that you were an apple tree,
you blossomed small and you bore fruit when you grew up,
the northern wind blew and shook off the apples.'

Also very popular is a motif of the dead as a tree that was cut down[176]:

Ποιος ήταν κείνος πόβανε φωτιά ' ς το περιβόλι
κ' εκάη η φράχτη ταμπελιού, κ' εκάη το περιβόλι,
κ' εκάησαν τα δυό δεντρά, που ήσαν αδερφωμένα; (Politis 188)
Who was the one who put the fire in the orchard
and the fence of the vineyard burnt and the orchard burnt,
and the two trees, which were closely joined, burnt?

In this context, Charos appears to be the figure of a reaper, a harvester who gathers unripe crops:

Σταράκι μου καθαριστό κι αγουροθερισμένο,
Που σ' αγουροθερίσανε του Χάρου οι θεριστάδες.[177]
My little wheat, clean and prematurely reaped,
which was prematurely reaped by the reapers of Charos.

Ο κόσμος είναι ένα δεντρί, κ' εμείς το πωρικό του
ο Χάρος είναι τρυγητής και παίρνει το ανθό του.[178]
The world is a tree and we are its fruit
Charos is a harvester and he gathers its flowers.

θερίζεις νέον και γέροντα, κόρην και παλλικάριν.[179]
You reap the young and the old, girl and boy.

It is noteworthy that, as a Reaper, Charos very rarely uses a scythe or a sickle, which in popular imagination have always been linked to the personification of death. We come across this kind of attribute almost exclusively in folk songs from Crete, the Dodekanese and Lesvos, namely from those islands that through the centuries were under strong West

[176] Bzinkowski 2011a: 446. The motif of comparing the dead and a tree is common in demotic poetry. See especially Roilos 1988: 61–85. See also Borowska 2008: 79–80.

[177] Cited by Alexiou 2002b: 197.

[178] Cited by Omatos 1990: 310.

[179] Cited by Omatos 1990: 310.

European influence.[180] Right there, an image, so well-known from the medieval representation of Death and so well rooted in the collective memory and exploited throughout centuries in hundreds of paintings, has been preserved, that is of Death with a scythe – an image completely unknown in Byzantine art and literature.[181]

There are just a few examples in Modern Greek folk songs where we deal with the motif of a scythe or a sickle (δρεπάνι means both of them). For instance, in some songs from Karpathos, Lesvos and Zakynthos[182]:

> Και πιάνει το δραπάνι του και βάλλει το σπαθίν του. (Manolakakis 95)
> *And he seizes his sickle and puts his sword.*

> Ου Χάροντας ου άγριους που αίματα βυζάνει,
> Θέρισι του παιδάκι μου μι του σκληρό δριπάνι. (Darakis, p. 63)
> *Charos, the wild one, who suckles blood,*
> *he reaps my little child with a hard sickle.*

> Δραπάνι έχει στο χέρι του, πέφτουν τα κόκκαλά του. (Schmidt 37)
> *He had a sickle in his hand, his bones fall down.*

These scant examples of Charos equipped with a scythe occur in songs originated in the area that was subjected to the influence of the people that appeared in Greece during the Frankokratia.[183] It seems that the images of death, known as the Triumph of Death (*Trionfi della Morte*) of Italian origin,[184] must have exerted a sort of influence in places subjected to Italian culture transmitted to Greek islands together with

---

180 Anagnostopoulos 1984: 76 ff.

181 Hesseling (1931, 131) mentions a didactic poem found by Moravcsik (1930) in a thirteenth-century manuscript in the Vatican Library. There we come across a very interesting fragment, obviously of western origin, where there is a mention of Charos' "sickle," yet here in its ancient Greek form (τὸ φάσγανον): τῷ φασγάνῳ δὲ τῷ μακρῷ καὶ καμπύλῳ.

182 Alexiou knows only one song with a mention of Charos' sickle. Alexiou 1978: 227; 234. Dawkins 1942: 143 mentions two fragments with a scythe, one from a folk song from Karpathos, the other one from *The Plague of Rhodes* of Emmanuel Georgillas.

183 Saunier in the archive of ΚΕΕΛ (Ύλη Πολίτη 198, 5, 6) found a song from Lefkada, where instead of the verb κουρσεύει, we come across the version κοσεύει, of Slavonic origin, where kosa (κόσα, κοσσιά), namely a scythe used for reaping crops is concerned. According to him, it is undoubtedly the influence of West European images of Death. Saunier 1982: 305. See also Dawkins 1942: 143–144.

184 Vovelle 2008: 132–136.

Venetians.[185] Although the way of cultural transmission seems rather understandable, the way these images of Charos with a scythe found their way to demotic poetry is completely obscure and – I would dare say – unidentifiable. Moreover, Death was imagined in the West at least from the fifteenth century as a skeleton wielding a scythe, an image that we will not find anywhere in Greek songs.

Although Charos in folk poetry is never personified in the West European way as a skeleton, a theme known in medieval and also popular in Baroque representations,[186] we come across such an image in the Cretan Renaissance tragedy Erofili by Chortatsis. Charos himself speaks in the prologue, threatening by his appearance, which undoubtedly brings characteristics of a non Greek origin[187]:

> Ἡ ἄγρια κι ἀνελύπητη καὶ σκοτεινὴ θωριά μου,
> καὶ τὸ δραπάνι ὁποὺ βαστῶ, καὶ τοῦτα τὰ γδυμνά μου κόκκαλα… (v. 1–3)[188]
> *My appearance is wild and merciless,*
> *and the sickle I keep in hand and these naked bones…*

This prologue and West European characteristics of Charos were used some centuries later by Pavlos Klados (Παύλος Κλάδος), a priest from Arachnes in Crete in his poem *Address to Death and Religious Advices* (Αποστροφή προς τον θάνατον και θρησκευτικές συμβουλές), written in 1712.[189] He accuses Death/Charos of the evil he brings to people:

> Τζι ανθρώπους όλους σφάζεις και σκοτώνεις,
> γιατί με το δρεπάνι σου τζι σώνεις.[190]
> *You slaughter and kill all the people,*
> *because you finish them with your sickle.*

---

[185] Bakker – Van Gemert 2008: 55.

[186] Białostocki 2007: 82.

[187] Omatos 1990: 308.

[188] Alexiou, Aposkiti 1988: v. 1–3.

[189] Makromichelaki 2011: 473.

[190] Παύλου Κλάδου, Αποστροφή προς τον θάνατον, Έκδοση Χρ.Ν. Πέτρου-Μεσογείτου ΕΕΚΣ Β' (1939), σ. 355. The same Charos' attribute is mentioned once in Erotokritos but in a completely different context: Στην κεφαλή είχε ολόμαυρον τον Χάρο με δρεπάνι, Β 361.

In Gioustos Glykys' from Koroni *Mourning for Death* (*Πένθος θανάτου, ζωής μάταιον και προς Θεόν επιστροφή*), written in 1524[191] we find the same description:

Και το δρεπάνι οπού βαστάς, καθώς σε ζωγραφίζουν.
And the sickle you keep, as they paint you.[192]

It is noteworthy that similar characteristics of Charos appear in an account of the plague on Rhodes in 1498, known as *The Plague of Rhodes* (*Το Θανατικόν της Ρόδου*) written by Emmanuel Georgillas (Εμμανουήλ Γεωργιλάς). Apart from the allusions to *The Second Coming* known from fourteenth- and fifteenth-century wall-paintings, it contains many elements of Charos-Death as a Reaper, for instance "naked arms" (τα γυμνά τα πράτσα σου) or "the sickles" (τα δρέπανά σου).[193]

The question of why in Greek islands, where we find folk songs with a motif of Charos the Reaper, there is no single mention at all about the motif of Death as a skeleton is still pending. However, it is worth remembering that such representations – of Charos with a scythe standing straight – are very rare, but exist in post-Byzantine paintings that we could find in the Catholic churches of Crete, such as the Church of the Dormition of the Mother of God in Gournia in Crete (Ναός της Κοίμησης της Θεοτόκου).[194]

---

[191] Knös 1962: 311.

[192] Cited by Omatos 1990: 310 who follows *Πένθος Θανάτου*. Νέα Ελληνική Βιβλιοθήκη, Αθήνα 1988, 270 ff. Knös suggests Glykys might have seen the wall-paintings containing such a motif in Koroni. Knös 1962: 312. There were also some other works on the Underworld theme from that period, among others: *Speech of the Dead King* (*Ομιλία του νεκρού βασιλιά*) written before 1513 or *Rhyme concerning Death* (*Ρίμα περί του θανάτου*), written before 1493. Van Gemert 1991: 67.

[193] Alexiou 1978: 225–226. The whole passage: "Πολλοί σε ζωγραφίσασιν και κάθεσαι επάνω/ – αμμή εγώ θωρώντα σε είμαι δια ν' αποθάνω/ και αν σκιαστόν τρομάσσω σε να' σαι σαν τον τρομάρχην-/ επάνω εις τον Κέρβερον σατανοδιαβολάρχην,/ πρόσωπον ξενοχάραγον, κορμίν και όντα πράγμα,/ με τα γυμνά τα πράτσα σου, να πη δεν σώνει γράμμα,/ τες ευμορφιές και κάλλη σου τα έχει η βασιλειά σου/ κρατών πασίλογ' άρματα και με τα δρέπανά σου" (210–217).

[194] Bakker – Van Gemert 2008: 54. There are also some examples in churches in Sifnos or in the Gregoriou Monastery on Mount Athos. Anagnostopoulos 1984: 76.

Merchant, Peddler

I will outline the idea that life can be redeemed and death may be postponed later in the chapter about the motif of *charopalema*. In the Cappadocian version of the motif, Charos appears to be a merchant or a peddler and the encounter with him turns into a trade meeting. The theme, as Saunier convincingly proves, might be associated with the historical pirate attacks that Greek coasts were continuously exposed to for centuries.[195] Thus, he categorizes some songs that, according to him, are supposed to be connected with piracy into a group he calls "unachievable redemption" (ανέφικτη εξαγορά). In my opinion, associating all the songs containing the "redemption" motif with pirates is groundless and needs to be verified.

First of all, Charos is called a pirate (κουρσάρος) very rarely and often this designation is accompanied by another word, for instance a peddler (πραματευτής),[196] secondly, there is no evident connection with the "redemption" motif and Charos' activity as a pirate. Definitely, the question of some gifts or money that could be used to plead with Charos to let someone free has no connection with some oral formulas in which he appears as a pirate, which I shall try to prove below.

The attempt of the redemption of the dead[197] from Charos is the main theme of some songs cited by Saunier in the chapter above. I shall deal only with the songs containing direct allusions to Charos, omitting those where he is absent, which constitute the greater part of the selection. As it turns out, Charos is very rarely mentioned in the context of redemption.

The motif may appear in the form of a young man pleading with his wife to redeem him from Charos (Saunier 3β, p. 200)[198] or the anony-

---

195 Saunier 1999: 189 ff.

196 See above the chapter "Charos' general characteristics".

197 Another variant of "redemption from Hades" might be, as I suppose, the recurring motif of "catching Charos" that we come across occasionally. Usually, some young dead people try to catch Death/Charos and is some cases even "to hang" him or to make him a slave: Το Χάρο τον επιάσανε και παν να τον κρεμάσουν (Pasayanis 4; 83), Το Χάρο τον επιάσανε και σκλάβο τονε πάνε (Pasayanis 5). Saunier 1979: 324–325.

198 In some of the songs a motif of Charos' wife and Charos' children appears. See below the chapter "Charos' family."

mous begging of someone dead (Saunier 3α, p. 198). In a version from Pontus, a young man, supposedly dead, asks his mother to take care of him because Charos had arrived at their house on his horse. Her answer disillusions him as for the possibilities to avoid the unavoidable (Saunier 4, p. 200).

As Saunier notes, one of the most widespread versions throughout Greece within the framework of this motif[199] is a group of songs in which a mother asks Charos to buy out her son from him (Saunier 7α, p. 204) and in some versions he answers he is not a "voivode" (βόιβοδας) nor accepts a tribute (χαρατσιάρης/χαρατζής, Saunier 7β, p. 204; Saunier 7γ, p. 206; Saunier 7δ, p. 206).[200] The reiterating formulas in many songs stress Charos' incorruptibility and, simultaneously, the inevitability of death:

> Χάρε μου δεν πληρώνεσαι, Χάρε μ' δεν παίρνεις γρόσια. (Saunier 7β, p. 204)
> *My Charos, you are incorruptible, my Charos, you don't take payments.*

> Χάρε μου, δεν πληρώνεσαι και δεν παρακαλιέσαι. (Saunier 7γ, p. 206)
> *My Charos, you are incorruptible and implacable.*

Charos leaves no doubts for those who beg him to let them out in exchange for money. As he confesses:

> εμέν με λέν πραματευτή, που πραματεύω κόσμο. (Saunier 7δ, p. 206)
> *They call me a peddler, because I peddle people.*

Another variant of the motif of redemption, which – in my opinion – should be considered separately because of evident discrepancies in comparison with those presented above, is the motif of Charos selling the dead.

In some songs that Saunier regards as exclusively Peloponnesian,[201] an oral formula of "Charos is selling me" appears (μένα ο Χάρος με πουλεί/πουλάει, Saunier 5α, 5β, p. 202). In these versions, a dead young man asks his wife or someone beloved to find some gifts for Charos to pay for his return to the world of the living. One of the things demanded

---

[199] Saunier 1999: 205.

[200] Interestingly, in this song Charos was identified with "the black earth" (Είμαι η μαύρη γης) that "eats" the living. As for the motif of the "Black Earth," see below the chapter "Charos' wedding."

[201] Saunier 1999: 203.

by Charos turns out to be the sun (ο ήλιος), which, of course, is very symbolic in the eschatological context and brings many associations circulating around the pair of light-darkness. However, the sun constantly revolves (τρυγυριστής, Saunier 5α, p. 202) or is "unbearable to look at" (ατήρητος, Saunier 5β, p. 202) and thus the payment is not possible.

Another variation of the analysed motif is selling the dead at the bazaar (στο παζάρι),[202] the image that undoubtedly may be connected with pirates and the abductions they must have committed, as Saunier rightly supposed.[203] Yet, Charos is not present in this context, nor do we find any allusions to him.

I would say that there is no need to seek the possible interpretations of the motif in historical events. This is a symbolic representation of the conviction common to all mankind that death is unavoidable and neither gifts nor money will be sufficient to buy oneself out. Interestingly, the intensification of such a concept is clearly visible in medieval art and literature, almost obsessively based on death themes and *memento mori* maxim. I would suggest that, together with the above-mentioned motives of Charos the Reaper and partly the Hunter, his representations as a peddler or merchant may also go back to medieval West European concepts. Of course, the universality of the motif can indicate it is something we could also find in other mythological traditions. Yet, it is worth underlining that Byzantine medieval tradition, art as well as literature, was not interested in the representation of death in the context of money. It was much more spiritual than its Catholic version in West Europe. Thus, it seems probable that such a concept that we find in *mirologia* – not so often really – might have originated, as the other elements, from a different tradition that was in constant contact with Greek lands.

---

[202] In fact, it is the name that is being sold: το όνομα πουλιέται στο παζάρι (Saunier 6, p. 202). In many cases, instead of the mention of someone dead (νεκρός), we come across in demotic songs his equivalent as "a name." For instance: "whose was the name that has been carried away by the river" (Τίνους ήτανε τ' όνομα, που πήρε το ποτάμι;/ – Δικό μας ήταν τ' όνομα, που πήρε το ποτάμι!, Matsinopoulos Δ-1, β'). The name in other versions may be taken by the sun and melted (το πήρε ο ήλιος κι έλιωσε, cited by Matsinopoulos 2008: 205).

[203] Saunier 1999: 203.

Chapter III

CONTEXT

1. Wrestling or playing with Charos

In this chapter, I set out to compare different versions of acritic songs containing the archetypal motif of "a man wrestling with Death."[204] The analysis of selected variants of the songs from the Pontus region, Cappadocia, Cyprus and the Ionian Islands reveals evident discrepancies in the use of the motif of struggle with Death/Charos and – in my opinion – questions both the common origin of the analysed variants as well as the coherence of their categorization as a separate group.

One of the most meaningful mythological motives appearing in all traditions from prehistoric times, represented in arts and literature, it also naturally permeated to folk tradition. In Modern Greek folk songs, it is reflected in the so-called motif of *charopalema* (χαροπάλεμα), literally "fighting" or "wrestling with Charos." Interestingly, the mythological concept found its continuation in the language, which I have already mentioned above, where the term has a common meaning as "the struggle preceding natural death."[205] In this context, the folk songs based on this motif or alluding to it may be regarded as a mythological pattern for this kind of universal human experience.

---

[204] The motif has been analysed meticulously by Politis in his introduction to the collection of acritic songs containing the songs of "death of Digenis." Politis 1909: 169–207. Still the most important in this matter is a paper by Saunier (Saunier 1972: 119–152; 335–370).

[205] See the chapter "Charos in Modern Greek language."

In Modern Greek folk poetry, we come across two kinds of such songs. One group constitutes countless, and widespread in every corner of the Greek mainland, songs about wrestling with Charos-Death that we could call an encounter of a young man (λεβέντης) or a shepherd (τσοπάνης) with Charos.[206]

The story, regardless of many differences in particular variants, has many common recurring features. A carefree shepherd who descends from the mountains is spotted by Charos who sits on a high rock. They start a conversation and Charos confesses that he has been sent by God himself to take the shepherd's soul. The shepherd refuses and proposes a fight, the result of which is always predictable because Charos is invariably the winner. However, the conquered shepherd begs Charos to postpone his death, arguing that he has a lot of duties at home (wife, children and animals).[207]

As has already been convincingly proved, this type turns out to be not original but derivative and was adapted from acritic songs. In this regard, the protagonist of these songs would constitute a counterpart of the hero of acritic songs, Digenis Akritas, who in the folk imagination of agricultural society metamorphosed himself into a shepherd to suit the rural reality.[208]

We should remember, as I have already noted, that – although medieval Greek folk songs were not widespread in the Greek mainland[209] – we can find some traces of them in their more recent adaptations and variants, which are hidden under the textual layers and imagery[210] sometimes going back further in time and provoking questions about their possible sources. As most scholars nowadays suggest, acritic songs

[206] Alexiou 1978: 227–228. Borowska 2008: 79–81. The versions of the song we find, for instance, [in:] Politis (214, Του Λεβέντη και του Χάρου; 215, Του Χάρου και του νιου; 216, Του Χάρου και του στραθιώτη); EDT (129, 130, 132); Kougeas (46, 88); Kapsalis (628); Matsinopoulos (Δ-4, α', β'); Motsios (69, 70); Kriaris (243); Nimas (1 A'-Θ'); Theros (677–680). Saunier, who analysed 128 variants of the song, discovered that the theme is unknown on Crete, Cyprus and in inland Asia Minor and the place of origin of the songs with this motif is probably in the regions of Epirus and Macedonia. Saunier 1972: 144.

[207] Saunier 1972: 144–148.

[208] Stathis 2004: 771–772. Politis A. 2011: 76. Alexiou 1978: 228.

[209] Alexiou 1978: 230.

[210] Politis A. 2011: 75.

are not supposed to be of medieval origin and most of them could have been written during the nineteenth century[211] and the term itself is an invention of the folklorists.[212] According to some of them, the proof of their later composition are the songs about the achievements of Digenis that have no connection at all with the epic of Digenis Akritas,[213] as – for instance – the motif under consideration, namely the fight of Digenis with Charos, does not exist in any of the manuscripts and variants of the epic.[214]

In this chapter, I venture to compare different versions of the second group of folk songs with the motif of the meeting of a man with Charos, namely, their acritic versions. Firstly, to show a variety of variants that differ greatly, secondly, to pay attention to intercultural influences determined by the place of origin of a given song, and lastly to attempt to elucidate some eschatological problems appearing together with this motif.

The question of hypothetical sources has already been researched, but so far has not reached a satisfying result.[215] Saunier distinguished four original types of the motif, dividing them into two acritic, two non acritic and thirteen derivatives containing fragments of the original versions.[216] My purpose is not to undermine the proposals and conclusions

---

211 Saunier 1972: 121.

212 Alexiou 2002a: 205–206. Alexiou notes that the main theme of acritic songs is the premature death of a young man. See also Saunier 1979: 287–302.

213 Beaton 2004: 78–82.

214 Hesseling 1897: 23. Saunier 1972: 121. Bzinkowski 2009: 24. We come across the name in its ancient version as "Charon" (Χάρων) in a version from the monastery of Grottaferrata (8.2, 8.125, 8.269) as well as in the variant of the epic known as Escorial (vv. 1794, 1795), but in both versions he has nothing in common with Charos from demotic songs and he appears rather as a simple synonym to death. The statement of Hutter, Sikke in their paper that this was one of the most popular episodes from the epic is obviously groundless. Hutter, Sikke 1979: 62.

215 Alexiou 1978: 227–229. Alexiou herself admits that there are serious discrepancies between Eurypides' Alkestis – with the fight with Thanatos over Alcestis' soul – that she regards as a source of modern combat with Charos and the modern version of it. In my opinion, her suggestion as to any dependence of the Modern Greek version on the ancient prototype is completely devoid of basis. Alexiou 1978: 229. For ancient origins of the motif, see also Stathis 2004: 777.

216 Saunier 1972: 119–152, 335–370. He also added a group with a common theme of "Bet of Giannis with Ilios [the Sun]" (Στοίχημα Γιάννη και Ήλιου). Saunier 1999: 537.

of the researchers but hopefully to add something that, I suppose, lacks in the hitherto research. I would describe it as a perspective pertaining the structure of the narratives as well as their content and context. Moreover, while analysing the present motif, it seems to me essential not to forget about the possible West European influences that might have been exerted on Modern Greek versions of the representation of fighting with death.

a) Pontic type – on the copper threshing floor (χάλκινον αλώνιν)

The Pontic type has a subsequent narrative structure: Akritis[217] builds a castle or a tower – a motif I will deal with in the following chapters – but the birds that so far had sung about his happiness, suddenly start to foresee his imminent death. Akritis goes hunting but, instead of prey, he encounters Charos at a crossroads. It is noteworthy that the crossroads bring here mythological associations, for they allude directly to the place of passage to the Netherworld.[218] However, Charos is not a stranger, he seems rather an old acquaintance. The protagonist of the song accuses Charos of bothering him all the time and challenges him to a duel:

Έλα, Χάρ', ας παλεύωμεν στο χάλκινον τ' αλώνιν,
Χάρε, και αν νικάς με εσύ, να παιρς και την ψυχήν μου,
Χάρε, και αν νικώ σ'εγώ, να χαίρομαι τον κόσμον. (Saunier, 1, p. 538; Politis b, pp. 234–235, 24)
Come, Charos, let's fight on the bronze threshing floor,
Charos, if you conquer me, take my soul,
Charos, if I win, let me rejoice the world.

In Markos' collection containing two songs of this type, the difference in the form of the battle concerns the last element, which is the bet, in this case Charos' black horse itself – an element I have already spoken about above:

For more about the *charopalema* motif, see Anagnostopoulos 1984: 119–120. Lawson 1910: 104. For a comparative analysis, see Saunier 1972 and Stathis 2004: 771–784.

[217] In the Pontus region, the hero is never called Digenis. Moreover his name "Akritis" was changed into "Akritas" by Sathas and Legrand who discovered the first manuscript of the epic of Digenis. Beaton 2004: 78.

[218] Stathis 2004: 773.

Χάρε μ', γιά 'λα ας παλεύουμε 'ς το χάλκενον τ' αλώνιν,
ας εν' και το νικάς μ' εσύ, έπαρ' την ψή μ' και δέβα,
ας εν και το νικείεσαι, θα παίρνω και το μαύρο σ'. (Markos, p. 176; 178 Ακρίτας κάστρον έχτιζεν)
Charos, let's fight on the bronze threshing floor,
if you win, take my soul and go away,
if I win, I will take your black horse.

In Politis' version, the last element of the bet are soul and life[219]:

και αν νικάς με, Χάροντα, να πάρης τημ ψυχήμ μου,
κ' εγ' αν νικώ σε, Χάροντα, να έχω τημ ζωήμ μου. (Politis b, pp. 251–252, 40; see also Politis b, pp. 245–246, 35)
And if you conquer me, Charos, take my soul,
and if I win, let me keep my life.

Worth underlining is the lack of a significant element – there is no mention of any weapon used by the fighters. Besides that, we even don't know either how they fought or any details of the combat that has an expected result, for Charos always turns out to be the winner.[220]

Εξέβαν και επάλεψαν, ενίκεσεν ο Χάρον. (Markos, pp. 176, 178; see also Saunier, 1, p. 538)
They came out and fought, Charos won.

The fragments cited above clearly show that in Pontic versions the motif of the fight does not exist and the only thing we can see is its result. Anyhow, if we look at the analysed scene from a higher perspective, we would discern some very interesting characteristics. Without forgetting the Pontic peculiarities, we could describe the scene as follows: a lonely horse-rider goes hunting and meets another one at the crossroads, starting a conversation with him. In turn, they bet on what they get if either of them will conquer the other one. I am convinced that right here we should try to seek any possible sources of the Pontic *charopalema* motif.

The context of the Pontic version indicates we are dealing here with the same motif I have already mentioned while analysing the figure of Charos as a hunter: the medieval motif of an encounter with Death. Al-

---

219 The end of this version is somehow surprising, because the winner here is Akritas and Charos is killed. Politis suggests the text should be corrected. Politis 1909: 246. See also Alexiou 1978: 228.

220 Saunier 1972: 127.

though there are no such texts in Byzantine literature, we can find them in the texts written in demotic Greek in the last years of Byzantium, known as *Alphabetical Dialogues of man and Charos/Death* (Διάλογοι κατά αλφάβητον ανθρώπου και του Χάρου), which resemble and undoubtedly were inspired by West European medieval "Dialogues of man with Death," which I have mentioned above.[221]

In the Pontic version, there is also one feature that, in my opinion, might be – although as a remote association – linked to medieval representations of Death. All the above scene could be described as a "game with Death" rather than a "fight." As it turns out, there are some medieval paintings, yet not so frequent, depicting that sort of facing death according to medieval concepts. The best known example is a wall painting by Albertus Pictor (c. 1440–c. 1507) in Täby Church (Täby kyrka) near Stockholm, the one that inspired Ingmar Bergman in his allegorical famous film *The Seventh Seal* (*Det sjunde inseglet*, 1957). The scenery in Bergman's film is astonishingly similar to that of the Pontic version of the analysed motif, which indicates that we are dealing somehow with a universal, even archetypal figure. A knight returning from the Crusades to Sweden encounters Death – by the way in a black cloak, similar to the representation of Charos as a man dressed in black – and challenges him to a chess match, which Death accepts and they start playing – the bet in the game is the knight's life.

If we suppose that the Pontic version of *charopalema* is just an expression of the universal idea of a man fighting with Death and reflects the conviction that even the unavoidable may be conquered by a mere game, the fight with Charos would be seen as nothing more than just a Greek version of an archetypal image.

b) Cappadocian type – on the marbles

The songs from Cappadocia – the place historically connected with the Akrites, the guards of the Eastern borders of the Byzantine Empire[222] – seem to be a variant of the Pontic type. However, the protagonist here, the name of whom is yet unknown, purposely builds a tower, so that

---

[221] Hesseling 1931: 133. Omatos 1990: 306–307. Panagiotakes 1995: 311–313.

[222] Saunier 1972: 336–337.

Charos could not find him.[223] Similarly, in this type of motif in question, there are some variants in which we won't find any mention of the combat with Charos/Death. Instead of it, there are some features that tend to underline the fact that: life can be redeemed and a man can postpone the unavoidable (like in the case of Akritas' wife who, instead of 40 days, understood she would be given 40 years of life by Charos).[224]

As a matter of fact, Charos in the Cappadocian version turns out to be a merchant, a peddler,[225] though merciless in his demands as for the payment that belongs to him, yet trustworthy. Consequently, the fight with Charos in Cappadocian songs turns into a trade meeting during which both parties agree on the conditions and terms of the contract.

In this regard, as I suppose, realizing that it may seem just another remote and groundless association, we could once more look for some possible traces in the medieval West European representations of Death we have already seen above. The allegorical representations known as *Danse Macabre*[226] allude directly to the kind of meeting of Death with a merchant.[227] Naturally, in Cappadocian songs the man is not a merchant, but it is Charos himself, however, one cannot help feeling that both images might have a common origin in archetypal thinking. Regardless of who the merchant is, the point of the meeting is life itself that, according to medieval concepts, is not redeemable.

Anyhow, the characteristics of Charos as a merchant are too few to definitely, without hesitation, link the image to the medieval concept. In the Cappadocian versions some features of Charos as a merciless conqueror appear, the concept I have already considered and which is probably more vital in Greek folk tradition than his supposed "commercial" activity:

> [...] απ' τα μαλλιά τον έπιασε ' ς μάρμαρα τον βάζει.
> Χάρε μ', άφες μ' ας τα μαλλιά και πιάς' με ας το χέρι,
> ή δείξε με την τέντα σου μονάχος μ' ας πηγαίνω. (Politis b, p. 247, 36. Sinassou; see also Saunier 2, p. 540, from Lagarde's collection)

223 Saunier 1999: 541. As for the tower motif, see the chapter "Charos the builder."

224 For the exact survey of different variants, see Saunier 1972: 337–341.

225 See the chapter "Charos' specific representations," part "Merchant, Peddler."

226 Hesseling 1931: 134.

227 We see this kind of representation in almost all versions of late-medieval allegories known as the Dance of Death, like in Hans Holbein's woodcuts drawn in 1526.

[...] he caught him by his hair and threw into the marbles.
Charos, leave my hair and take me by the hand,
or show me your tent so that I could go there by myself.

In a version cited by Politis, which he took from the earlier collection of Lagarde (1886), some characteristics appear that show the encounter with Charos in Capaddocian versions as a real fight. It is noteworthy that Charos' weapons mentioned here, a spear (κοντάρι) and a sword (σπαθί), are completely unknown elsewhere.[228]

Politis suggests that it might be Akritas' wife who encourages the opponents to fight, yet Lagarde thought it was rather Akritas' mother speaking to her son.[229] In this variant the motif of "pulling the hair" is significant – the sign of Charos' atrocity or just a symbolic representation of taking vital powers from a man – and the mention of a tent that we also come across in the songs of the Shepherd and Charos.[230] It is also worth noticing that the characteristics of Charos as "reasonable" (φρόνιμος) and "well-educated" (κάλλιο παιδευμένος) may indicate a Christian "intrusion" and the need to describe Charos as a good servant of God, a motif we don't find in any other version as far as I know[231]:

Ας πάρη Ακρίτης το σπαθί, και συ, Χάρε, το κοντάρι,
εβγάτ' εκεί 'ς στο πόλεμο, 'ς ένα πλατύ λιβάδι.
Νούτον ο Χάρος φρόνιμος και κάλλιο παιδευμένος.
Έπιασε Χάρος το σπαθί, τζακίσθην το σπαθί του,
πιάσε κ' από κονταριού, τζακίσθην το κοντάρι.
Ας τα μαλλιά τον έπιασε, 'ς τα μάρμαρα τον κρούει.
'Χάρ', άφες μ' ας τα μαλλιά, και πιάσ' μ' ας το χέρι,
Για δείξε με την τέντα σου, και μοναχό μ' ας πάγω.' (Politis b, p. 248, 37)
Let Akritis take the sword and you, Charos, the spear,
go out to fight, on the vast meadow.
Charos was reasonable and well-educated.
Charos took the sword, his sword broke,

---

[228] Saunier notes that the text of all variants in this place is corrupted and confused. Saunier 1972: 339.

[229] Lagarde 1886: 26. Unfortunately, we don't know who the informants of Lagarde were or if the collector changed by himself the version of the song, which was very common practice then, as I have already mentioned, when the folk songs were regarded rather as a written than oral text. Beaton 2004: 203. In fact, there is no similar version of the song which rather suggests that it may not be genuine.

[230] Saunier 1972: 339–340.

[231] Saunier 1972: 239. Saunier 1979: 331.

he took his spear, his spear broke.
He took him by his hair, knocked him down on the marbles.
'Charos, leave my hair and take me by the hand,
or show me your tent so that I could go there by myself.'

c) Cypriot type – in the palaistra

The most elaborated versions with the motif of encounter with Charos come from Cyprus and are usually rather long compositions. The plot of the story follows a similar scheme: Charos appears during a feast and is invited by three young men to join them and eat and drink in their company. He refuses, explaining he has come to take the youngest of them, who – after a short dialogue – turns out to be Digenis himself. Then a fight with Charos takes place, which constitutes the most expanded version in comparison with any other containing the analysed motif. Yet, what is worth underlining, the motif of fighting with Charos is not the central one and not the most important in these versions. As it turns out, the main part of the narrative contains a story usually told by Digenis on his deathbed to his friends.[232]

The most significant features of the combat have nothing in common either with the Pontic or Cappadocian versions.

It is wrestling, without the use of any weapon, it lasts three days and three nights and the opponents fight not on a threshing-floor but in the palaistra:

Σερκές, σερκές επκιάσασιν και στην παλιώστραν πάσιν.
Τζαι τζει 'νι πουπαλιώννασιν τρεις νύχτες, τρεις ημέρες.
Τζει πο 'πκιανεν ο Χάροντας τα γαίματα πιτούσαν,
τζει πο 'πκιανεν ο Διγενής τα κόκκαλα ελειούσαν. (Saunier, p. 542, 3; Politis b, p. 210, 1; Markos p. 180, Πάνω στες έξη του μηνός; Kitromilidou, p. 16, 2; see also Politis b, pp. 212–214, 2)
They caught themselves hand by hand and went into the palaistra.
And there they fought three nights, three days.
There, where Charos caught, the blood flew,
there, where Digenis caught, the bones were disjointed.

[232] In some versions, Digenis kills his wife at the end of the story because she had chosen Giannis instead of him when he dies. Alexiou 1978: 228.

The battle is unsolved, Charos transforms himself into a golden eagle and asks God for help, who in turn gives him a sort of divine power, which is called enigmatically "theoti" (θεότη)[233]:

Χρουσός ατός εγίνηκεν, στους ουρανούς τζ' εξέην,
τζ' άνοιξεν τες αλάτες του τζαι τοθ' Θεόδ δοξάζει.
[...]
Τζαι πκιάσε, πκιάσε, Χάροντα, τζαι τούτην τηθ θεότην,
του Διγενή την έδειξεν, τζαι ππέφτει στο κρεββάτιν. (Saunier, p. 542, 3; Kitromilidou, p. 19, 3; see also Politis b, p. 210, 1; Markos p. 180, Πάνω στες έξη του μηνός; Kitromilidou, p. 17, 2)
He became a golden eagle, flew to the heavens,
opened his wings and praised the Lord.
[...]
Catch, catch, Charos, this divine power,
Charos showed it to Digenis and he fell into bed.

Politis cites another Cypriot version that differs significantly in this point, at least seemingly. After the first clash that brought no result and meant that Charos was obliged to call for God's help, the narrative changes, assuming some elements from Christian eschatology:

Ήρτε φωνή που τον θεόν κι' από τους Αρχαγγέλους.
'Και δεν σε πέμψα, Χάροντα, παλιώματα να κάμνης,
παρά στειλά σε, Χάροντα, ψυχαίς για να μου βκάλλης.'
Χρυσός ατός εγίνηκε πάνω 'ς την κεφαλήν του,
κ' έσκαπτεν με νύχιν του να βκάλη την ψυχήν του.
Κι' ο Διγενής ψυχομαχεί σε σιδερά παλάτια,
σε σιδερά παπλώματα, σε σιδερά κρεβάτια. (Politis b, pp. 212–214, 2)
There came a voice from God and from the Archangels.
'I haven't sent you, Charos, so that you fight,
but I have sent you, Charos, so that you take out the souls.'
He became a golden eagle over the head of Digenis,
and he dug with his claw to take out his soul.
And Digenis is dying in his iron palaces,
in his iron sheets, on his iron beds.

Irrelevantly, if Politis, inspired by the older collections, especially by Sakellarios (1868) and Legrand (1874), had created the above-mentioned version himself, the whole fragment seems to be composed of

---

[233] Saunier rightly notes that the abstract term θεότη belongs to scholar language and consequently to the learned tradition. Saunier 1972: 135. Similarly, Politis was puzzled by this noun and confessed he had no idea what it meant. Politis 1909: 211. For more, see the chapter "Charos and the Angels."

different variants with the addition of two rather seldom elements, appearing in this context: a reproach of God towards Charos for not executing his duties and a mention of the Archangels. I shall deal with the problem of angelology in demotic songs in the next chapters. In this place, it is sufficient to say that Charos is identified sometimes with the Archangel Michael, playing the role of *psychopompos* in folk tradition, which I shall elaborate subsequently.[234]

d) The Heptanesian type – jump competition

In Heptanesian versions of the encounter with Charos we find a motif completely unknown anywhere else, namely a jump competition. Whereas in other variants, it was Digenis fighting with Charos, here it is a "widow's son" (ο γιος της χήρας). Moreover, they build the castle "somewhere in Jerusalem" (κάπου στα Γεροσόλυμα) – the element also known from the Pontic versions – which is constructed purposely so that people could hide themselves and Charos would not find them. Likewise in the Cypriot versions – he enters during the feast and states he has come to take the best of them. Consequently, the youngest one, who turns out to be the widow's son, answers and challenges Charos to compete in a jumping competition:

> Χάρο, ας παρασαρτάρουμε, κι' όποιος προλάβει ας πάρει.
> Σαρταίν' τση χήρας το παιδί, πάει σαράντα πάσσα
> σαρταίν' ο Πρικοχάροντας και πάει σαρανταπέντε.
> Σαρταίν' τση χήρας το παιδί και πάει πενήντα πάσσα,
> Σαρταίνει ο Πρικοχάροντας και πάει πενηνταπέντε. (Saunier, p. 560, 9β; Politis b, pp. 256–257, 46, Kefalonia; see also Schmidt 20)
> *Charos, let's compete in jumping, and who will be further, he wins.*
> *The widow's son jumps, he reaches forty steps,*
> *The Bitter Charos jumps, he reaches forty five.*
> *The widow's son jumps, he reaches fifty steps,*
> *The Bitter Charos jumps, he reaches fifty five.*

Saunier drew this song from Schmidt's collection (1877),[235] who – contrary to his contemporary folklorists – is regarded rather as one

---

[234] Lawson 1910: 45;101. Omatos 1990: 307. Krueger 2006: 91, 125. Bzinkowski 2009: 27.

[235] Politis classifies this song as acritic, rewriting the notes of Schmidt that the first five verses are sung only in the village of Skala.

who meticulously and thoroughly wrote down the songs he heard during his stays on Zakynthos, Kefalonia and Ithaca.

Saunier cites another two songs of this kind in his collection. The first one he took from Tomasseo (1842)[236] and it differs only in two elements: the widow's son is mentioned by name, he is called Giannis, and the competition takes place on the *marble threshing floor* ('ς τα μαρμαρένια αλώνια, Politis, pp. 257–258, 47). It is interesting to highlight this if we recall that in the Pontic versions the threshing floor was made of copper (χάλκινον) and in Crete usually of iron (σίδερο).[237] In the second song, from the island of Chios, the protagonist of the story is called Konstandis and unexpectedly he manages in the end to "knock Charos to the ground" (ρίχτει το Χάρω κάτω, Politis b, pp. 258–259, 48).

However, the most interesting aspect in this regard is a Heptanesian variant drawn by Politis from the collection of Kanellakis (1890). Here, instead of Charos, we come across another mythological figure known from folk tradition, Drakos, who provokes others to fight with him:

'Ποιος έχει σίδερο σπαθί, σίδερο βρακοζώνι,
ποιος έχει στήθος μάρμαρον, το Δράκο να παλαίση;'
'Who has the iron sword, the iron belt,
who has the marble breast to conquer Drakos?'

Only the widow's son accepts Charos' challenge:

'Ελα να πα πηδήσωμε εις τους ανήλιους τόπους.'
Πηδά της χήρας το παιδί τσαι πα εξήντα μίλλια,
Επήδησε τσ' ο Δράκος μας τσαι πα εξηνταπέντε.
'Σου τη χαρίζω τη ζωή, να σαι ξεντροπιασμένος.'
'Come, so that we jump in sunless places.'
The widow's son jumps and he reaches sixty miles,
Drakos jumps and he reaches sixty five.
'I spare your life, so that you regain your good name.'

This variant, besides the features mentioned above, contains an interesting name of the place the competition takes place, which is *sunless places* (ανήλιους τόπους),[238] bringing to mind eschatological connota-

[236] Tomasseo draws some folk songs from the poet Donysios Solomos. Beaton 2004: 8–9.

[237] So far, I have not found any satisfying explanation of the differentiation of the material that the threshing-floor of demotic songs is made of.

[238] See the chapter "The Underworld of the demotic songs."

tions. Secondly, the fight with Drakos ends happily for his opponent, but not in the other versions:

> Κι' οχ τα μαλλιά τον έπιασε και τόνε κωλοσέρνει.
> 'Άσε με, Χάρε, αφ' τα μαλλιά και πιάσε μ' αφ' τα χέρια.' (Saunier, p. 560, 9β; Politis b, pp. 256–257, 46; see also Politis b, p. 258, 47)
> *He caught him by his hair and he dragged him.*
> *'Charos, release my hair and grasp my hands.'*

> Ο Χάρος ήτο πονηρός τσ' αφ' τα μαλλιά τον πιάνει.
> 'Άφις με, Χαρ, αφ' τα μαλλιά, τσαι πιάσ' με αφ' το χέρι,
> τσαι δείξε μου το μέρος σου να πάγω μοναχός μου.' (Politis, p. 259, 48)
> *Charos was cunning and he caught him by his hair.*
> *'Charos, release my hair and grasp my hands,*
> *and show me your tent, so that I could go there by myself.'*

Saunier pays attention to the motif of "pulling the hair" known also from the Cappadocian versions, associating it with the motif of Charos the Pirate,[239] suggesting that it might reflect some historical events that took place in the Hellenic ground.[240] I wouldn't agree with his statement. It would seem unjustifiable and very risky to join mythological, one could say even archetypal, motifs present in folk songs with real events. It seems rather that it reflects the most archaic concepts connected with hair and death, like beliefs about vital powers that were supposed to be taken by pulling the hair in the moment of death[241] and also resembles some ancient ritual practices during which the hair of victims was cut.[242]

In my opinion, in the Heptanesian versions of *charopalema* motif, traditions and motives that originated in different epochs and in regions distant from each other conflated, creating such a specific image. Once more I can't get rid of the impression that, in the liveliness and mobility of the protagonists of the Heptanesian version competing in a jump-

---

[239] See the chapter "Charos nekropompos."

[240] Saunier pays attention to the usage of the word τέντα, which is of Latin origin and was used as a military term. Saunier 1982: 301–302. Moreover, it seems to interconnect with the motif of "pulling the hair" that we come across in the songs about the fight of a young man with Charos. Saunier 1972: 340.

[241] Stathis 2004: 780. Although his attempt to correlate the motif with the ancient idea of the external soul that we find, among others, in the Biblical story of Sampson is very alluring, in my opinion, it is not supported by any convincing evidence. Stathis 2004: 781.

[242] Omatos 1990: 309.

ing competition, one could notice some echoes of medieval dances with Death, similarly full of vitality and spontaneity in its grotesque form.

All the remarks made above allow me to put forward a suggestion that it would be groundless to categorize separately some songs into a group called "fight with Charos-Death." The differences between the versions regarding the way of fighting as well as the context clearly prove that the fight with Charos/Death constitutes merely one of the elements of the narratives, in any case the most important and leading one in the plot. However, the question as to what extent the eschatological images appearing in the cited songs reflect the medieval concepts of Death, or the archetypal, mythological, ahistorical and timeless prototypes, is still open to discussion.

2. Charos and the Angels

In this chapter[243] I focus on the well-known John Cuthbert Lawson's study about Modern Greek folklore (1910) and I venture to verify if it may be regarded as a reliable source of information about Greek folk beliefs. I base my argument on the eschatological remarks Lawson made concerning the personification of Death – Charos and his relationship with the Christian Angels. Confronting Lawson's views and his source material with other similar demotic songs, mainly from the collections he had access to, I try to show how the older collections of folk songs might have distorted or falsified the eschatological images of Charos and the Angels, and what he overlooked while analysing the sources. I also shed some light on the possible influences of Byzantine Orthodoxy on Modern Greek folk tradition to which Greek demotic songs belong.

One of the books that has been an inexhaustible source of information for over a hundred years concerning the supposed continuity of ancient Greece in its modern counterpart is a memorable study by a young classical scholar John Cuthbert Lawson (1874–1919), a Fellow

243 The whole chapter is an almost unaltered version of my recent paper (Bzinkowski 2015a).

of Pembroke College in Cambridge, entitled *Modern Greek Folklore and Ancient Greek Religion: A Study in Survivals* (Lawson 1910).[244]

As the author writes in the preface to his book, he spent two years in Greece (1898–1900) thanks to the Craven Fund, which financed his stay and work that he undertook in order to gather the information for his research on the customs of modern Greece.[245] But the real purpose he aimed to achieve was not the ethnographic collection of data during the fieldwork, but – as he states with undisguised pride – the first attempt ever made to show modern Greek folklore as a significant and essential vehicle for the exploration of the continuity of Ancient Greek religion.[246]

The same year when Lawson's book was published, it was reviewed in *The Classical Review* by the then influential classical scholar Jane Ellen Harrison (1850–1928), who did not conceal her admiration for his work, but simultaneously reproached him for neglecting and rejecting the comparative method and not showing modern Greek folklore in a broader perspective in comparison with other primitive tribal initiation ceremonies.[247] Another critical insight into Lawson's book is offered by the review written the same year by H.J. Rose, who accused the author of being "childish" in interpreting the religious passages from ancient writers that he had no knowledge about at all.[248] On the other hand, Rose admits that the ethnographic data gathered by Lawson is indeed valuable and his remarks about the contemporary beliefs of Modern Greeks deserve credit.

Two years later, a Professor of Harvard University, Clifford Herschel Moore (1866–1931) later author of the classic study on Greek religion (Moore 1916) and translator of Tacitus' *Historiae*, reviewed Lawson's book, paying attention to the richness of the content concerning Greek folklore, as well as to the author's lack of knowledge of contemporary studies on Greek religion that could support his, in many cases doubt-

---

244 Other well-known studies by English visitors in Greece during the nineteenth and the beginning of the twentieth century include: Geldart 1884; Rodd 1892; Abbot 1903.

245 Lawson 1910: vii.

246 Lawson 1910: x.

247 Harrison 1910: 183.

248 Rose 1910: 529–532.

ful, theses.[249] According to Moore, one should also treat with caution the accounts used by Lawson, due to the fact that respondents' oral accounts are not always trustworthy.[250] However, the most critical review was published the same year by George L. Hamilton who explicitly reproached Lawson for his unacceptable ignorance of both comparative religions and folklore studies, as well as a complete lack of knowledge of the broader European context of the tales and folk stories he deals with in his book.[251] Later reviews, such as Johannes Th. Kakridis' detailed analysis of some passages in Lawson's book that are oversimplified or misleading,[252] or a short review by Américo Paredes[253] generally share the opinion that, although in many cases his study is obviously out of date, one must not deny his ability to show universal beliefs and practices.

The person most critical both to the question of the diachronic survivalism of Hellenic culture, and the person who sought every possible source that could explain modern tales via ancient myths, was a professor of Greek at the University of Oxford, archaeologist and folklorist, Director of the British School in Athens, Richard M. Dawkins (1871–1955). One of the most influential Neohellenist scholars, whose works,[254] thanks to his research accuracy and thorough documentation of the sources, are invariably admired in modern scholarship,[255] strongly stressed the necessity to see Greek folk tales in terms of a synchronic system where every element is meaningful for the community that is an addressee of a story.[256] Instead of tracing back modern folklore to ancient Greek culture, he preferred the comparative method and sought

[249] Moore 1912: 108–111.

[250] Moore 1912: 111.

[251] Hamilton 1912: 87–90. For instance, he observes that Lawson does not know either the then well-known collection of folk tales by Hahn (1864), or Dyer's study about Greek religion (Dyer 1891) that could support some of his theses and place them in their relevant context.

[252] Kakridis 1969: 495–499.

[253] Paredes 1965: 356.

[254] The most influential are: Dawkins 1916, the result of three visits to Cappadocia (1909, 1910, 1911) just before the Balkan wars began, and Dawkins 1953.

[255] Alexiou 2002a: 218.

[256] Mackridge 2009: 56; Tziovas 2014: 26, n. 5.

to juxtapose Greek folk songs with their counterparts in other contemporary cultures.[257]

Since Lawson's study, in spite of the lapse of time and change of approaches, is regarded, among others by Alexiou in her influential monograph,[258] as a still reliable source of information about Greek folk beliefs, in the present chapter I venture to verify this statement. Based on the eschatological remarks Lawson made concerning the personification of Death in Greek tradition and specifically the relationship between the pagan Charos/Death and the Christian Angels, I will try to establish the degree to which his account may be up-to-date and if the information he conveys on the subject is up-to-date or if it should be disregarded. Thus, confronting Lawson's views and his source material with other similar demotic songs, mainly from the collections he had access to, I shall try to show in what way the older collections of folk songs he used might have distorted or falsified the eschatological images of Charos and the Angels, and what he overlooked while analysing the sources. Simultaneously, I also hope to shed some light on a problem that, in my opinion, is rather neglected by researchers of Greek demotic poetry, namely the possible influences of Byzantine Orthodoxy on Modern Greek folk tradition, to which Greek demotic songs belong.

It also seems useful to pay some attention to the sources of Greek demotic songs Lawson used to illustrate his theses about Modern Greek eschatology. He cites, among others, the collections of Passow (1860) and Schmidt (1877), and mentions the works of the founder of Greek folk studies, Nikolaos Politis (1852–1921), whose first Greek collection of songs he could not have known for obvious reasons.[259] It is also

---

[257] Mackridge 2009: 56. In a letter to Hasluck, Dawkins writes that Lawson "does not possess an imaginative mind. It's odd that such an unsuitable person got hold of such a subject" (Dawkins to Hasluck, 2 Feb. 1919). The quote is from Mackridge 2009: 56. However, later he seems to have softened his stance against Lawson. For instance, in the James Frazer Memorial Lecture given at Oxford on 5th May in 1924, although he does not agree with Lawson's opinion about the vampires, he shares his views on the eschatology of Greek dirges. Besides this, he also shares some of Lawson's views about the continuity of ancient Greek concepts about the afterlife of an individual. See Dawkins 1942: 134–136.

[258] Alexiou 2002a: 455, n. 24.

[259] The first edition of the well-known collection was published in 1914. Interestingly, when publishing his collection, Politis used the method of textual criticism

worth remembering that, at that time, other collections of Greek songs in translation into European languages were already plentiful in England,[260] France[261] and Germany or Austria.[262]

However, what is extremely interesting and – as I suppose – has not attracted proper interest so far, in spite of Lawson's peculiar attitude to folk elements and his tendency to link every similar element with ancient Greek sources, is the fact that he is fully aware of the "double-faith" patterns of Greek folk beliefs based, on the one hand, on Christian elements as the legacy of the Byzantine Church and, on the other, on Hellenic sources of ancient origin.[263] As he notes, with a sort of perplexity, peasants seem not to bother and easily identify both sides of their beliefs.[264]

Undoubtedly, Lawson is right in his general supposition that the Modern Greek Charos is only partly what Charon used to be in clas-

---

that he borrowed from the classical studies. Moreover, in contradistinction to European folklore studies of that time, Greek folk songs were treated mostly as "written text" and their oral performance was neglected. See especially Alexiou 1984–1985: 7–10.

[260] See above the chapter I "Sources." A detailed list and comparison of the nineteenth-century European collections of Greek folk songs was made by Ibrovac (1966: 153–248) and if one would like to check any relevant information I strongly recommend his thorough study. As for the Greek collections and their relationship to European sources, see Politis A. 2011: 277–283, 325–334. For a short survey of collections, see also Beaton 1986: 115–117. Here I mention merely some of the English collections Lawson might have known and could have had access to. Apart from the translation of Claude Fauriel's collection by Sherridan (Fauriel 1825), collections by Garnett (1888) and by Abbot (1900) were already available.

[261] The most important are these by Marcellus 1851; Lévy 1860; and especially by Legrand 1874. See Ibrovac 1966: 187–188.

[262] The most influential, it seems, was the anthology by Karl Theodor Kind that had four editions (1835, 1844, 1849). In the last one published in 1861 (*Anthologie neugriechischer Volkslieder*) Kind used the earlier collections and excerpted some songs from them: among others from Passow, 1860; Zambelios 1852; Tomasseo 1842. See Ibrovac 1966: 212–213.

[263] Bzinkowski 2011: 104–105. See also Dawkins 1942.

[264] Lawson (1910: 53, 101) even suggests that Charos is – though rarely – called ἅγιος (saint). I have not found so far any confirmation of his statement either in collections of demotic songs or in the studies devoted to the subject. Thus, I omit this remark in my analysis.

sical times,[265] namely the carrier of the dead to the "Homeric"-looking Underworld,[266] although, as it should be stressed, he is by no means "the ferryman" but rather a "psychopompos," as documented elsewhere.[267] Generally, in accordance with the method he chose and the goal he aimed to attain, Lawson regards Charos simply as "an ancient deity."[268] The speculation whether the name of the modern personification of death in Greek tradition is indirectly rooted in the name of the ancient ferryman, Charon, does not engage him so much. He limits himself just to a statement that the origins of this modern deity are taken for granted and the case does not need more elucidation.[269] This is a significant way of treating the researched material by the scholar who seems to have chosen the shortest path to reach the confirmation of his theses. In other words, that some manifestations of Modern Greek folk customs are an indirect continuity of the ancient rituals and beliefs that survived on Hellenic ground in spite of the domination of Christianity. It is worth noticing because it reveals the core of his methodology: to see ancient features in everything that seems similar but to omit the differences and, more importantly, not to take into account the transitional stages of the development of a researched feature. However, let us remember that it was not uncommon for nineteenth-century European scholars, for whom Greek folklore was interesting, provided that it could be linked to the classical past and possibly explain ancient Greek mythology or religion.[270]

Moreover, the case of Charos touches upon the question of the credibility of the accounts that gave Lawson the proof material for his research. As he states, the interlocutors asked about the personified death

---

[265] The whole chapter about Charos, see Lawson 1910: 98–117. Abbot (1903: 205–207), who mentions Charos only in the context of funeral rites, is also aware of the complexity of a division of his duties and unclear origins.

[266] As for the Modern Greek Underworld and its relation to Ancient Greek Hades, see the chapter "The Underworld of demotic songs." See also Dawkins 1942: 143–145.

[267] Lawson 1910: 98. For the outline of his role as a psychopompos see, among others, my paper: Bzinkowski 2009. In the present book, I present the question in the chapter "Charos nekropompos."

[268] Lawson 1910: 98.

[269] Lawson 1910: 98.

[270] Alexiou 1984–1985: 9.

showed “neither superstitious awe nor fear,”[271] which demonstrates that he did not take into account the facts obvious for all ethnographers and researchers working on the spot. Firstly, the respondents’ attitude to strangers does not allow them to speak openly, especially when the question is a ritualized taboo of a village or a traditional society, and that is exactly the case of death as it is a “border situation.” Secondly, the informants just do not want to show they are superstitious or backward.[272] On the other hand, the respondent, in order to show himself and the story in a better light, may embroider it to make it more attractive or simply provide information that is expected.[273] It could also be the case, which Abbot suspects, that Lawson had known that the informant simply did not remember exactly the story or the song he cited and thus changed its contents.[274]

Thus, the knowledge that Lawson gathered while investigating the inhabitants of Greek villages must be treated very cautiously and attempting to reconstruct the folk beliefs based mainly on the accounts he refers to would be quite risky. Besides this, it was not the main aim of the scholar who – as I have already mentioned – attempted to show the relics of Ancient Greek religion by shedding some light (though in some cases rather obscuring than illuminating) on the possible reminiscences or traces of its manifestations in folk customs and beliefs.

* * *

Lawson suggests that in some cases Charos, who “is conceived to be a free agent responsible to none or merely a minister of the supreme God,”[275] is accompanied in his duties by God’s assistants, the Angels.[276]

---

[271] Alexiou 1984–1985: 9.

[272] Alexiou 1984–1985: 12–13.

[273] Alexiou 1984–1985: 11.

[274] Abbot 1903: 206.

[275] Lawson 1910: 101.

[276] It would be a difficult task, as I suppose, to find an equivalent image for instance in Byzantine texts. Byzantium had never developed a coherent and universally accepted system of the spiritual existence of the Angels. Besides this, it had never rejected Biblical ideas and more ancient concepts about them. Apart from pseudo-Dionysius the Areopagite’s *Celestial hierarchy*, who distinguished nine orders of the angels according to Neoplatonic concepts, there is no other Byzantine treatise dealing thoroughly with the

Their duty in the version of a demotic song mentioned by him and taken in turn from Passow's collection, is to take care of children during the journey to Hades. Interestingly, the motif comes from a very popular song that we come across in almost every part of Greece,[277] *Charos and the Shepherd* or *The Young Brave and Charos* (*Ο Χάρος και ο Τσοπάνης*, *Του Λεβέντη και του Χάρου*) that corresponds to different versions of the song belonging to the acritic cycle, *Digenis and Charos*.[278]

Interestingly, in Passow's version, after the fight, which was in a sort of a scheme of "wrestling with Charos" (χαροπάλεμα), the shepherd that had surrendered ordered Charos to take him to his tent: δείξε μου την τέντα σου να πάγω μοναχός μου ("and show me your tent so that I go by myself").[279] Charos' answer gives no hope and rather aims to make the shepherd realize his situation:

> Να δγης εσύ την τέντα μου, ο τρομιασμός σε πιάνει,
> Οπώχω τα μικρά παιδιά που φέρνουνε τ'οι Αγγέλοι. (Passow 427)[280]

---

problem of angelology. See Meyendorff 1979: 136. What is striking in Dionysius' system is that those who are in direct contact with humanity are angels and archangels who are at the bottom of the angelic hierarchy, whereas in Byzantium the case of Archangel Michael indicates that the folk beliefs in him were rooted rather in pagan and Jewish concepts than in theologians' treatises. See Peers 2001: 5–6 – a remarkable, hitherto most comprehensive study of Byzantine angelology.

277 Dawkins 1942: 136.

278 See the previous chapter "Wrestling with Charos." Here, let me recall that the heroic medieval songs mostly were not disseminated in mainland Greece. However, the versions of the songs with a motif of wrestling of a young brave (λεβέντης) or a shepherd (τσοπάνης) with Death/Charos are the traces of the *charopalema* motif of Digenis Akritas. They were adapted to a new reality, namely to the agricultural society. See Politis A. 2011: 75–76. Lawson (1910: 104) knows a Cypriot version of such a song from Sakellarios' collection. For more on different versions of the motif, see Anagnostopoulos 1984: 119–120. For the comparative and cultural analysis, see Saunier 1972 and also Stathis 2004: 771–784. Saunier (1999: 537) also includes in this group a third category: "A bet between Yannis and the Sun" (Στοίχημα Γιάννη και Ήλιου), which, according to him, is a different form of the motif of wrestling with Death.

279 Saunier (1982: 301–302) convincingly suggests that it is a strictly military term and he directs attention to the historical background of the motif. It is striking that Dawkins (1942: 136) misinterprets this passage and writes that the one conquered in the struggle with Death "must dwell in Charos' tent." In the cited fragment it is obviously the shepherd's will to go there.

280 We find the same fragment in an almost unaltered version in Kind's collection, no. IX (Ο Χάρος και ο τσοπάνης), p. 76: Να ιδής εσύ την τέντα μου, ο τρομασμός σε πιάνει,/ Οπώχω τα μικρά παιδιά, που φέρνουν οι Αγγέλοι.

When you see my tent, you will be filled with dismay,
Just there I have the little children, the ones that the Angels bring me.

Interestingly, the parallel examples do not exist in demotic songs (at least I have not found any other similar ones so far), which means that the image of the Angels helping Charos in his duties by taking children may be something extremely incidental, or there must be another explanation of the appearance of the motif.[281] There is no such mention in Fauriel's collection, although it contains a version of the song "The Shepherd and Charos" (Fauriel II, 90–93).[282] Neither do we come across it in

---

[281] Stathis (2004: 776), basing on Θρησκευτική και Ηθική Εγκυκλοπαίδεια (12 volumes, edited by A. Martinos), refers to that: "The angels take the souls of small children and they bring them to Charos" (οι Άγγελοι παίρνουν τις ψυχές των αθώων παιδιών και τις φέρνουν στο Χάρο). Due to the fact that I had no access to Stathis' source, it is impossible for me to verify his statement. However, I realize that such a conviction may be rooted in folk Orthodox beliefs and the problem definitely needs a separate research procedure. There are also some accounts in Psychogiou that may confirm the eschatological connection between the angels and children in folk tradition. Psychogiou 2008: 303, according to Eleni Psychogiou, age 80, illiterate: Τα μικρά παιδιά, άμα πεθαίνουνε αβάφτηγα, ούτε τα διαβάζουνε ούτε το θάβανε μέσ' στην εκκλησία [στο νεκροταφείο]. Τα βαφτισμένα τα θάβουνε με πολλά λουλούδια και τα λένε «οι άγγελοι του θεού» ("When little children die unbaptized, they are not read out nor buried in church [in the graveyard]. The children that are baptized, they bury with a lot of flowers and they call them "the angels of God"). Psychogiou 2008: 319, according to Anna Rozaki, age 55, literate: όταν είναι [ο νεκρός] μικρό παιδάκι, μέχρι 10–12 χρονών, φτιάχνομε κουλουράκια σε σχήμα γ που τα λέμε 'λαζάρους' και τα μοιράζομε και λέμε 'οι αγγέλοι να του τα πάνε' ("When a small child [dies], around 10–12 years of age, we make bagels in the shape of the letter gamma, we distribute them and we say 'may the angels bring them to him'").

[282] Almost the same version is contained in Abbot's collection. Another collection Lawson might have read, namely the well-known anthology by Legrand (1874) contains only a few songs about Charos and the Underworld that do not contribute at all to our issue. Interestingly, both Abbot and Legrand abundantly drew from earlier collections of folk songs, but they never made reference to them. See Politis A. 2011: 266. Only in the anthology of Kind (1861) do we come across another mention of the angels, though – I daresay – even more obscure and rather unusual in demotic songs. In a variation of a well-known song about Charos the builder, who builds the orchard (garden) from dead bodies, in the first part, which is rather impossible to connect to the second one with the well-known motif, there is a phrase that seems to be obviously an intrusion: μα εκείνος ήτον άγγελος με ταις χρυσαίς φτερούγαις ("But he was the angel with the golden wings"). See Kind 1861: 68, song V (Το περιβόλι του Χάρου). It cannot be easily determined whether it is about Charos identified here with The Angel of Death or if

the collection by Iatridis (1859), known and cited by Lawson, in which a variant of the story appears under the title: Ότι ουδέν αδάμαστον απέναντι του αδυσωπήτου θανάτου (Τραγώδι παλαιότατον) (Iatridis 16–18) nor in Chasiotis, who mentions two variants of the song (Chasiotis 167–168).

Besides this, in the collection of Passow there are other songs centred around the motif of "Death and the Shepherd," but the Angels do not appear. Instead, in the case of our fragment and its parallel versions, we are dealing with a strictly formulaic language: the second part of a verse is replaced by different elements while the first one stays (almost) unchanged. Let us cite some examples of the above-mentioned formula to see the oral technique of composition:

> Μωρέ αν δγης την τέντα μου, όλος ανατρομάξεις. (Passow 428 [the last verse of the song])
> *You fool, if you see my tent, you will be wholly scared.*
>
> Να πας κ' ιδής την τέντα μου θέλεις να συντ'ομάξεις
> Διατ'είν' απόξω π'άσινη και μέσα μαυ'ομένη. (Passow 432)
> *When you go and see my tent you will be scared*
> *Because from the outside it is green, from the inside black.*
>
> Πάμε να δεις την τέντα μου να στραβοκατινίσης.
> Απόξ' έχω τα κόκκινα και μές'έχω τα μαύρα. (Passow 433; Kind, nr VII [Ο Ζάχος και ο Χάρος], p. 72)
> *Let' s go, so that you see my tent and doubt.*
> *Outside I have red colours and inside black ones.*

We come across an interesting variation of the same formula in a collection that Lawson knows and cites several times, namely in folk songs from the island of Chios by Kanellakis (1890). In the Chiotic version of the song about Charos and the Shepherd (In Kanellakis': Τσόμπανης και Χάρων, no. 78, pp. 108–109) we do not find the cited formula, but there is another curious trace of Christian beliefs interweaving with the folk paganism. When, after the fight, Charos at last seized the shepherd's soul, he asked if he "had stolen any lambs or had eaten goats" (έκλεψες αρνιά; τσοπάν', ήφαγες 'γίδια). After the shepherd's negative answer his soul "was put on the scales and he went out justified" (Σ' την ζυγαριάν

it comes from another song not related to that one at all. As for the motif of Charos building the garden, see Stathis 2004: 801–806.

τον έβαλαν και ήβγεν δικηωμένος). Such a mixture of eschatological motives coming from two mutually exclusive worlds is found extremely rarely. The Netherworld of modern Greek demotic songs is generally "morally neutral" and there is no division of the dead according to their life's deeds.[283]

However, we come across the above-mentioned formula[284] in another song in Kanellakis' collection, entitled *Charon* which tells the story of three brothers building a tower in order to avoid Death/Charos, who unfortunately takes notice of them. Although they invite him to drink and eat with them – a motif frequently occurring in different variations throughout Greece – he stands to fight with Konstandis in a *charopalema*. The conquered Konstandis asks Charos to show him his place so that he could go alone there. He receives the following answer:

Να δης εμόν το μέρος μου τρομάρα θα σε πιάση,
'που 'ν' από μέσα σκοτεινό τσ' από 'ξω 'ραχνιασμένο
με των αντρών της τσεφαλαίς το 'χω εγώ χτισμένο
με των κοπέλλων τα μαλλιά το έχω 'σκεπασμένο. (Kanellakis, nr 35, p. 46)
As soon as you see my place, you will be scared,
because inside it is dark, outside cobwebbed
and I built it from men's heads
and covered it with girls' hair.

We encounter another variation of the motif in the collection of folk songs from Asia Minor by Lagarde (1886).[285] In a song from Cappadocia, the motif of *charopalema* differs in the character of Charos, who here is astonishingly "sensible and better educated" (φρόνιμος και κάλλιο παιδευμένος). Akritas, as in other versions, wants to go to Charos' tent alone, but he is warned by him[286]:

Αν σε δείξω την τέντα μου, πολύ θενά τρομάξεις,
ως κλώθει ολοπράσινα και μέσα ροχιασμένα,
ως κλώθουν τα τεντώματα, παλληκαριού βραχιόνια. (Lagarde, nr 22, p. 26)

---

[283] See the chapter "The Underworld of demotic songs".

[284] Interestingly, the cited formula appears very rarely in later versions of the song in twentieth-century collections as if it was regarded as a fragment coming from another narrative.

[285] The song is cited by Saunier in his collection of *mirologia* (Saunier 1999: 540).

[286] There are many variants of the song as well as of the formula. See Politis, Akritika, 247.

If I show you my tent, you will be very scared,
because around it is totally green from outside but inside it is cobwebbed,
because the arms of the young brave are stretched all around.[287]

It seems to me that the presence of the Angels in Passow's collection, mentioned in the first example as an illustration of Lawson's suggestion, could be explained in two ways. We should remind the reader indeed that Passow cites the song at second hand for he uses the older popular collection of Greek songs by an Italian linguist of Dalmatian origin, Niccolò Tommaseo (1802–1874), *Canti popolari italiani, corsi, illirici, greci* (Tommaseo 1842).[288]

Based on the comparison of the above-mentioned verses with parallel examples from similar songs, we could assume that the phrase as a part of a formula could have been introduced by a singer, who presented the song to Tomasseo, in order to satisfy the collector with a slight but significant reference to Christianity, replacing the phrase with "the Angels." Of course, I realize the lack of firm basis for such a supposition and thus I propose a second possibility. Tomasseo himself might have replaced the phrase he had heard and made it more "Christian" in the way that, instead of cruel and merciless Charos, he introduced the Angels, but only in one context – the one of carrying the children to the Underworld. Let us underline the fact that is neglected by other scholars commenting on Charos' presence in demotic songs. For, as it turns out, Tomasseo is fully aware of the possibility that the mention of the Angels may be a sort of intrusion and, according to him, no matter what the reality is, it is a good reason for rejoicing.[289]

---

[287] Due to the doubts about the meaning that arises with the last line, I decided to paraphrase it.

[288] For more on Tomasseo's collection, his sources of Greek songs, see Ibrovac 1966: 231–232. As we know, some of Tomasseo's informants were scholars and they purposely changed the songs they presented to Tomasseo to make them more elegant or more – in their opinion – proper. A very interesting example is one of the *Kleftic songs* alluding to the time before the War of Independence cited by Fauriel (t. 1, Του Κίτσου, p. 119) who had noted it from an anonymous informant. Because it was in prose, Fauriel gave it only in his French translation. However, slightly later, a teacher of The Flanginian School in Venice, Anthimos Mazarakis, changed Fauriel's prose translation into verses and transmitted it as a genuine song to Tomasseo, who published it in his collection. See Politis A. 2011: 183.

[289] Let me cite the passage from Tomasseo's collection to show my supposition more accurately: "L' imagine degli Angeli rallegra Il luogo dell' ultima notte. Non so se sia ver-

Thus, Lawson's remark that was a starting point for asking a question about the validity of the syncretistic connection between Charos and the Angels gains another dimension. Although Lawson had the possibility to collect the material on the spot, he chose, among others, Passow's collection that, in turn, was based on the texts published – let us say – in a scholarly manner. It is now well-known that Passow had the tendency to conflate some variants of the songs in order to – just like the classical philologists, the editors of ancient texts, used to – create the established model text of a given song based on all accessible versions.[290] Besides this, as it turns out, most of the collections of folk songs that were published in the nineteenth century were not the reproductions of oral performances at all, but the work of a scholarly mind organizing and readjusting the text material.[291] Thus, naturally we must also treat with great suspicion Lawson's remarks about the Angels in the company of Charos based on the cited folk songs.[292]

Interesting, though at first sight striking, is the information Lawson gives about Archangel Michael who, according to him, in some cases acts as a counterpart of Charos and plays the role of a *psychopompos* taking the souls to the Underworld.[293] Unfortunately, the scholar who

---

so intruso; ma toccarlo non oso: che mostra il confondersi delle cristiane tradizioni con le pagane, e quelle più liete. – Dicono il Cristianesimo malinconico! Il Cristianesimo trae gioia dal dolore; il Paganesimo dolore da gioia. L' uno dice: godiamo alla disperata, chè il dolore è inevitabile; l' altro dice: speriamo gioie sempre maggiori dell' inevitabil dolore" (Tomasseo 1842: 303). It is known that some of the "folk" songs in Tomasseo's collection were provided to him by the national Greek poet Dionysios Solomos, who never visited the Greek mainland and was interested in the creation of national Greek literature rather than the folk poetry itself. See Beaton 2004: 8–9.

290 Beaton 2004: 10, 203. Politis A. 2011: 256–257.

291 Beaton 2004: 203.

292 Interestingly, in one of the accounts in Psychogiou we come across such a company of Charos and the Angels. Syncretism of the image is explained by Psychogiou as a possible result of the sex of the narrator, who in this case is a man. Psychogiou 2008: 343, according to Theophanis Papoutsis, age 74, shepherd: Αχ ο Χάρος κάνει μια χαρά – αχ μωρέ μια χαρά/ μαζί με τους αγγέλους ("Oh, Charos has a good time, together with the angels").

293 Lawson 1910: 101. It seems that Dawkins (1942: 135–136) had not noticed this remark since he writes that "of the archangel we lose sight entirely; his place is taken by Charos." However, later he adds: "it is hard to say who the conductor of the dead is, Charos or the angel."

regards the Archangel as a natural Christian continuation of the ancient Hermes *psychopompos*[294] does not reveal where he drew his information from, nor does he give any example of a folk song or folk tale that could possibly illustrate that phenomenon. His main interest lies in juxtaposing the above-mentioned *charopalema* motif with a motif of "struggling with an angel" that, according to Schmidt's study, which he cites several times,[295] is reflected in the phraseology of Modern Greek,[296] so as a consequence he puts Archangel Michael aside.

As it turns out, Lawson is generally right in his remark about the presence of the Archangel. He indeed acts like Charos,[297] but – I would like to emphasise – this happens only in some specific cases.[298] What is yet more important is that I doubt if, as Lawson states,[299] he leads the souls to the Underworld.[300] Therefore, in my opinion, he is not interchangeable, as Lawson postulated, with Charos in all his duties as one

---

294 Lawson 1910: 45. He gives an example of a relic of ancient beliefs in the Maina village, where, according to him, people tell the story about the archangel with a sword passing at the mouth of the caves of Taenarus, exactly the same place where Heracles was supposed to come out with Cerberus.

295 Schmidt 1871: 230.

296 There are many terms describing the struggle with the angels, such as: αγγελοσκιάζουμαι, αγγελομαχώ, αγγελοκρίνομαι, αγγελοκριτηρεύομαι. See Anagnostopoulos 1984: 120f; Dawkins 1942: 135. I also referred to them in my paper: Bzinkowski 2009: 28.

297 Dawkins (1942: 136) recalls that in some folk songs we can find a reflection of the pictures of Michael we could see in church, where he is dressed in bright garments and is equipped like a Roman soldier. Charos similarly is sometimes, not frequently, presented as a shining warrior.

298 Anagnostopoulos 1984: 122–127.

299 Lawson 1910: 101.

300 In Psychogiou 2008 we find an interesting account about the angel in the Underworld. Psychogiou 2008: 338, according to Makri Aleksandra, age 80, illiterate: Λένε ότι πήγε μια φορά η Παναΐτσα με τον άγγελο στον Άδη, να ιδεί τσι ψυχούλες και τσι είδε να βασανίζονται και ρώτησε τον άγγελο και της είπε ο άγγελος τις αμαρτίες ("They say, once upon a time, the Mother of God together with the angel went to Hades to see the souls and saw that they are being tormented and asked the angel and he told her about the sins"). As it turns out, there are countless sources of the story about the visit of the Virgin Mary in the other world that survived in Greek, Ethiopic, Syriac, Arabic, Latin, Irish, Georgian, Armenian, Slavonic and Romanian languages that confirm the extraordinary popularity of Mary's katabasis. See Baun 2007: 16, 97–98. About the plot and the structure of the story, see Lambakis 1982: 46–49. Dawkins (1942: 133) mentions he had found an unpublished sixteenth- or seventeenth-century manuscript from the

would like him to be.[301] The folk songs in which his name appears exclude such a possibility, which I shall try to prove subsequently.

It is beyond the scope of this book to develop the subject of the presence of Archangel Michael – the patron saint of Byzantine emperors appearing on coins together with them – in Byzantine as well as in Orthodox art, where he manifests himself in thousands of icons and is an object of the greatest worship.[302] This confirms that he must have been important for all the believers of the Orthodox Church and, thus, naturally could have also permeated into the folk beliefs.

Instead, firstly let me point out that during the Byzantine era Archangel Michael had already been confused and identified with Death/Charos.[303] In the late Byzantine period, there are many paintings depicting the deceased accompanied by Archangel Michael, who had been regarded as the "escort of souls"[304] in the early Christian tradition that

Marcian library in Venice with a unique Cretan version written in Latin characters of the *Apocalypse of the Virgin*, containing many unusual motifs of the narrative.

301 Herzfeld (1982: 96), for example, cites a Cypriot scholar Loukas, who regards the Modern Greek Charos and the Archangel Michael as the same person with the same responsibilities. In the Escorial manuscript of Digenis Akritas, a dying hero is scared when seeing "The Angel of fire, descending from heavens" (Άγγελο πυρός, από ουρανού επελθόντα) and he cries to his wife: "Can you see, my dear, the angel who wants to take me?" (Βλέπεις, καλή, τον άγγελο οπού με θέλει πάρει;). The fragment of the Escorial version (verses 1765–1771) I cite from Stathis 2004: 775.

302 A miraculous icon of Archangel Michael on Lesvos, known as Archangel Michael of Mantamados, is very interesting in the eschatological context. He is also called "Arab" (Αράπης, Αραπέλλι) due to his black face and is presented rather as a hermaphrodite, which, according to Psychogiou, could indicate his strong connection to his chthonic character as a psychopompos and also relate to the androgynous "Black Earth" (Μαυρηγή) whom a dead (irrelevantly man or woman) symbolically marries. See Psychogiou 2008: 48.

303 Angold 2000: 445.

304 Krueger 2006: 125. As it turns out, there were even popular shrines of Archangel Michael (Krueger 2006: 91). The cult of Archangel Michael was also very widespread at Chonae, resulting in the popular tales of the miracle the archangel made at the shrine of his name there, dating back to the eighth century. See Peers 2001: 157f. It is also significant that, generally, the cult of the angels that flourished especially during the early Church became a problem for the Church because it was based mainly on a syncretic belief coming from Jewish and pagan traditions. See Peers 2001: 8.

we can find in the third-century apocryphal *Apocalypse of Paul.*[305] Numerous apocalypses from early as well as late Antiquity confirm that the cult of Archangel Michael was extremely popular in Byzantium.[306] Thus, there is no need to think, as Alexiou writes basing on Moravcsik,[307] that the hypothetical fusion might have originated in vernacular poetry of the late Byzantine period.[308] Until now, some people say, as Danforth notes, that forty days after death, the soul, after wandering about and visiting the people and places from its life, is presented by Charos to Archangel Michael (The Angel of the Lord), who eventually takes it to heaven (στους ουρανούς).[309]

The traces of confusion between Charos and Archangel could also be seen in the songs belonging to the acritic cycle, especially connected with different versions of the song *Death of Digenis* (*Ο Θάνατος του Διγενή*),[310] which Lawson fully realizes and in that case, rather unusually for him, gives his sources in the footnote.[311] The collections which he references contain a lot of interesting traces of the confusion of Chris-

---

305 Known also as *Visio Pauli* or *Visio Sancti Pauli* (ed. Tischendorf 1866). It presents the vision of heaven and hell seen by Paul the Apostle. See Baun 2007: 205–206. The relevant fragment of the "Apocalypse of Paul": "Let it [the soul] be delivered therefore unto Michael the angel of the covenant, and let him lead it into the paradise of rejoicing that it become fellow-heir with all the saints" (Paul 14, 43). "The Apocryphal New Testament," M.R. James (trans. and notes), Oxford 1924. Accessible on: http://wesley.nnu.edu/sermons-essays-books/noncanonical-literature/noncanonical-literature-apocryphal-nt-apocalypse/apocalypse-of-paul-summary/ (12.02.2015). About the plot as well as the characteristics of the story, see Lambakis 1982: 43–44.

306 Baun 2007: 205; Peers 2001: 157 f., chapter V: "Apprehending the Archangel Michael".

307 Moravcsik 1931: 45–61.

308 Alexiou 2002a: 216, n. 7.

309 Danforth 1982: 45. See also Angold 2000: 455–456. In ethnographic accounts the angel appears when someone is about to die soon. Psychogiou 2008: 307, according to Pigi Angelopoulou, age 72, illiterate: Όταν είναι κανένας να πεθάνει, κάπως αλλάζει, κάτι βλέπει, βλέπουνε τον άγγελό τους. ("When someone is about to die, he somehow changes, sees something, they see their angel"). The belief that in the moment of death the soul is taken by the angels and in particular by Archangel Michael is, according to Dawkins (1942: 135), a common folk belief.

310 Anagnostopoulos 1984: 122.

311 Lawson 1910: 104, n. 4. Lawson (1910: 102) also notes that even Charos was Christianised and the fact also influenced his character and made him more compassionate and, in some cases, even reluctant to fulfill God's orders.

tian motives with the pagan folk tradition. Both sources known to Lawson, Sakellarios (1891) as well as Politis (1909), provide examples of the coexistence of Christian elements artfully interwoven in the fibre of demotic songs (Sakellarios 1891; Politis 1909).

The biblical image of Archangel Michael with a sword in one hand and a scale in the other, very common in Byzantine iconography, has mingled with a folk personification of Death.[312] In acritic songs, which are regarded as the oldest preserved examples of demotic songs,[313] it seems that the subsequent fusion had not yet taken place. Let us see an example from Politis' collection which makes the issue of the responsibility for man's souls even more obscure. Digenis tells on his death bed a story about his adventures and brave deeds:

> Ποττέ μου δεν εδείλιασα ωσάν αυτήν την ώραν,
> που δα το Χάρον εγδυμνό, τολ Λιον αρματωμένο,
> τομ Μιχαήλ αρκάγγελο τριά σπαθιά τζωσμένο.
> το ένα ναι για τους φτωχούς, τάλλο για τους αρκόντους,
> το τρίτον το φαρμακερό για μας τους αντρειωμένους. (Politis b, p. 223, 8; Saunier 1999, 5β, p. 550)
> *I never feared like I do at that moment,*
> *when I saw naked Charos, armed Elijah,*
> *Archangel Michael belted with three swords.*
> *The one for the poor, the other for the nobles,*
> *the third, the poisoned one for the brave.*

Or in another song with the same motif of Digenis speaking before he dies:

> Κ'εκεί δεν εφοβήθηκα σαν τούτηνε την ώρα,
> που είδα το Χάρο ζωντανό, το Χάρο καβαλλάρη,
> που είδα τον αρχιστράτηγο με το σπαθί στο χέρι. (Politis b, p. 227, 14; Saunier 1999, 7α, p. 552)
> *I never feared like in that moment,*
> *when I saw Charos alive, Charos the rider,*
> *when I saw the archistrategos with a sword in hand.*

In Sakellarios' collection we come across another interesting, yet slightly different, example in the song entitled *The Alphabet Song of Charos* (*Άσμα το Αλφάβητον του Χάρου*):

---

[312] Anagnostopoulos 1984: 125.

[313] According to recent research, both the category of the songs and their medieval origins were questioned. See Politis A. 2011: 55.

Άρχοντες αδροικήσετε τ' αλφάβητον του Χάρου,
όταν ο Χάρος κη άθρωπος στέκουν και διαποντάρουν,
τον Μιχαήλ αρχάγγελον έχομεν σ' ταις δουλειαίς μας,
και την θεότην του 'δωκέν να παίρνη ταις ψυχαίς μας. (Sakellarios 7, p. 29)
You noble ones, you have heard the alphabet of Charos,
when Charos and a man stand and wrestle,
we have Archangel Michael for our affairs,
and it was given to him divine power[314] *[by God], so that he would take our souls.*

The aforementioned fragments clearly show the well-known phenomenon of syncretic beliefs and convictions manifest in the popular tradition of village societies. Folk imagination absorbed many elements not only from ancient, pre-Christian rituals and traditions, as we can see as one of the key-concepts in Lawson's book. It has also assimilated different concepts coming from different epochs and places and thus, from time to time, used to create images not exactly adherent or, one could say, not easily definable.

In the cited fragments we have different *psychopompoi*: Charos, Archangel Michael (also called Archistrategos)[315] and even Saint Elijah (here: Λιος).[316] However, the question of the correspondence between

---

[314] Politis (1909: 201), commenting on the word in the version of the song from Cyprus, is not sure what θεότη actually means: αγνωώ αν η λέξις έχει την έννοιαν εικόνος ή άλλου θείου πράγματος ("I don't know if the word has the meaning an image or any other divine thing"). See also the chapter "Wrestling or playing with Charos", part "Cypriot type".

[315] Baun 2007: 97, 391f. According to Jewish apocalyptic writings, including the Revelation, the archangels Michael and Gabriel are ranked just as "chief captains" of celestial armies, which seems to be the main source of their presence in the Byzantine liturgy. See Meyendorff 1979: 136. It stands in striking opposition to the concept of Pseudo Dionysius, where the archangels are the second rank from the bottom in the hierarchy of nine ranks. See Peers 2001: 4–5.

[316] Politis (1909: 190, 223) explains that in some regions of Greece Λιος is used as a diminutive of Εμμανουήλ, Μανώλης and probably it is an allusion to the prophet Elijah. According to Anagnostopoulos, it is certainly the Prophet Elijah who was taken to Heaven armoured (αρματωμένος). It is also worth noticing the strong connection between the prophet Elijah and Ilios (the Sun) due to the similarity of two words (Ηλίας – Ήλιος) that manifests in popular beliefs and is reflected in folk imagery. As for the connection between them in folk traditions, see Politis 1882: 45–54. The local tradition of Kerkyra also features Saint Spyridon who, according to Anagnostopoulos (1984: 123) acts like Charos (Chasiotis 1866: 177–178, no. 12). However, it seems to me that in this case the identification is impossible and it is due to a completely different context. In a song from Chasiotis' collection, the day of Saint Spyridon is approaching and thus

the persons mentioned above is not so easily tangible and I am not quite convinced – I dare say – if it is relevant at all. The core of the first fragment comes from a story that has countless variants throughout Greece about Digenis dying (Ο Διγενής ψυχομαχεί). If we look closer at the language and the imagery of the cited fragment, we will notice a formulaic expression[317] containing a tripartite enumeration (Χάρον – Λιον – Μιχαήλ) that corresponds in turn to the three swords of Michael which are assigned to each sort of the dead. We encounter the same situation in the next cited example, where a trio appears: Charos alive – Charos the rider – the Archangel with the sword.

The tripartite division into persons is, thus, an element of the expression characteristic for the oral tradition of composing the songs. I do not say definitely that it is meaningless but I try to cast some doubt on attempts at identifying what was sung (or written) and what is or was believed. I do not see in the cited fragment any signs of "cooperation" of the *psychopompoi* as some commentators suggest.[318] Neither could we see the presence of Michael or Elijah as a substitution or replacement of Charos.[319] The only conclusion that is visible more clearly after examining the language of the fragment is that we are dealing here with a process of "identification" or "fusion," using Alexiou's phraseology she used to describe in reference to the Modern Greek Charos.[320]

As a matter of fact, it is nothing more than what is called "the rule of three equivalents,"[321] the characteristic element of the morphology

---

a mother tries to plead with the saint, promising him some gifts if her beloved son could be alive. She blames Saint Spyridon for taking her child and regrets that instead of him there come birds, swallows, but he never comes back. In other versions, Charos' duties could be executed even by Saint Nicolas. See Anagnostopoulos 1984: 122–123. Politis (1909: 190) notes that the Saints as *psychopompoi* are rather unknown outside Asia Minor. Undoubtedly, the presence of the Saints executing Charos' duties needs a separate study and has not been, as far as I know, treated with accuracy and due attention by the scholars dealing with the subject of folk eschatology.

317 As for the formulas and their role in Greek folk songs, see especially Beaton 2004: 35–57.

318 Anagnostopoulos 1984: 122.

319 Anagnostopoulos 1984: 123.

320 Alexiou 1978: 224–225.

321 I use the term after Kosegian 2010: 33 (ο νόμος των τριών ισοδυνάμων). She argues that we find the motif of three equivalents already in *Homeric Hymns*, giving an

of Greek demotic songs that consists of expressing the same meaning in three different ways,[322] and more specifically introducing the main person as the third one and thus underlining his superiority over the others. In folk songs, this triadic scheme, which we can also come across in fables, as Alexis Politis notes,[323] may also be used to stress "the third, the best one" element of a whole,[324] but it may also indicate the general, symbolic usage of the number three, which is commonly used in different contexts of folk songs.[325]

Transferring these observations into the interpretation of the first two fragments cited above, we could say that Digenis sees Death that is polymorphous or, to put it more precisely, he sees the equivalent ways in which Death could appear in front of him – on the one hand, unknown, enigmatic and all-embracing, on the other, in the religious masks he could imagine and identify with Charos.

However, the third fragment, cited from Sakellarios' collection, diverts our attention in another direction. Here, Archangel Michael turns out to be the one who has the scale in his hands while a man fights with Death/Charos. He is the one that eventually takes our soul to heaven or not. As we read in a subsequent part of the same song in Sakellarios' collection, that is a sort of confession as well as pleading:

> Ω Μιχαήλ αρχάγγελε και πρώτε των αγγέλων
> 'που χαίρεσαι κη αγάλλεσαι μετά των αρχαγγέλων.
> Ω Μιχαήλ αρχάγγελε, πρόφθασε εις εμένα,
> και παραστάσου 'ς την ψυχήν γλυκά ταπεινωμένα.
> Ω Μιχαήλ αρχάγγελος γράφει τα κρίματά σου,

example of the *Hymn to Demeter* (13–14), where the following speak in turn: the sky, the earth and the sea, the three elements of the whole and thus the universe. See Kosegian 2010: 35.

322 Kosegian 2010: 33–36. Chara Kosegian cites a very figurative example of such a technique in the well-known song Της Λυγερής και του Χάρου. A girl, whose soul Charos is going to take, asks him to let her rejoice in the summer and see the ones who will come back from abroad. Apparently, she speaks about three different persons: her mother's son-in-law, her mother-in-law's son and her sister-in-law's brother – in reality about her husband. (Να 'ρτει της μάνας ο 'αμπρος, της πεθθεριάς μου ο υιος/ Της αντραδέρφης μ' αερφός κ' εμέναν ο καλός μου!). Kosegian 2010: 36.

323 Politis A. 2011: 153.

324 Kosegian 2010: 43.

325 Kosegian 2010: 56–59.

κη όντας σε πάρη 'ς τον κριτήν φέρνει τα ομπροστά του. (Sakellarios, no. 7, pp. 31–32)
Oh, Michael the Archangel and chief of the angels
who rejoice and enjoy together with the archangels.
Oh, Michael the Archangel, come near to me,
and stand by my soul mildly and humbly.
Oh, Michael the Archangel writes down your sins,
and when he takes you to the judge, he has them in front of him.

The confirmation of such a picture of Archangel Michael as a judge of the sins, of the one who holds the scale on which the human errors are weighed, we can also find in other demotic songs from different collections.[326] I shall cite a fragment of the *Song for Good Friday* (*Άσμα Μεγάλης Παρασκευής*) from a book that Lawson was supposed to know, which, however, is not clear because he does not refer to it, namely *The History of the Athenians* (*Ιστορία των Αθηναίων*) by Dimitrios Kambouroglou[327]:

κ' ο Μιχαήλ αρχάγγελος ο φοβερός και μέγας
όπου ζυγιάζει της ψυχαίς αμαρτωλαίς και δίκηαις.
And Michael the Archangel terrifying and great
he who weighs the souls of sinners and fair ones.

The Christian element of differentiating the souls according to man's life deeds and, as a consequence, allotting the soul to heaven or elsewhere has permeated into the almost entirely pagan eschatology of Modern Greek folk songs in which, as I have already mentioned, the Underworld is "neutral," like in ancient Homeric poems. However, such cases are very incidental and occur rarely in demotic songs together with other "Christianized" pagan ideas of mostly ancient origin.[328]

---

[326] Anagnostopoulos (1984: 124) gives interesting examples of such a motif.

[327] Kambouroglou 1889: 237. Anagnostopoulos (1984: 124) cites the same fragment from the later three-volume edition (Αθήναι 1959).

[328] To the best of my knowledge, so far there is no up-to-date study that would cover the question of the presence of Christian beliefs in the folk tradition of Modern Greece. An interesting and until now the best, as I suppose, approach has been made by Anagnostopoulos in his doctoral dissertation, especially in chapter 10 entitled "Η Κόλαση, ο Παράδεισος και η Μέλλουσα Κρίση" ("The Hell, the Paradise and the Last Judgement"). Anagnostopoulos 1984: 320–347. For the most recent and thorough study concerning the syncretism of Christianity and pagan folk elements, see Psychogiou 2008, especially 233–287 (chapter V).

Thus, once more trying to verify Lawson's knowledge about Modern Greek folklore that he included in his book, we observe the same tendency and the same method, which I would call a "unification of the similar, ignoring the differences, underlining the ancient origins." Although, as the mentions of books cited by him prove, he must have had access to contemporary collections and studies, his way of treating and examining the analysed material is rather negligent. The scholar cites the songs at second hand without critical insight into what he had read or heard during his field research. Along with the seemingly authentic accounts of the peasants he wrote down during his stay in Greece, his remarks reveal a somehow "romantic" folkloristic approach to popular religion[329] and a Philhellenic spirit that predisposes him to see all around him the ancient deities. It is by no means surprising if we take into account the stereotypical image of Greece that most of the West Europeans had through centuries.

The case of the appearance of the Angels among other elements of folk eschatology could constitute a good illustration of Lawson and his contemporaries' attitude to Modern Greek tradition, which is interesting provided that it comprises reminiscences of ancient predecessors. Moreover, the above-mentioned Angels and Archangel Michael also show clearly the ambiguous attitude towards Byzantine legacy and a rather reluctant view of the Medieval Empire that dominated over a thousand years in the Greek world. Edward Gibbon's well-known contempt of the Byzantines and their culture had influenced European minds for more than a century, and it is by no means surprising that the classically educated John Cutberth Lawson must have shared the same stereotypical opinion of the somewhat obscure Christianity of the Greeks. As a consequence, while presenting the Christian elements appearing in Greek folklore, he oversimplifies them and does not pay due attention to their relationship to popular beliefs deeply rooted among others in Byzantine iconography.[330] As for the examples he uses to illustrate his thesis about

---

329 Hartnup 2004: 8.

330 Moore (1912: 109) suggests that Lawson is generally right in his supposition that Christianity in the popular religion only applied some elements to the existent ones and modified some of the features belonging to the pagan religion. However, it seems more justifiable to share Hartnup's opinion that, in fact, just like other researchers of Lawson's

the continuity of Ancient Greek tradition, as I tried to show, the scholar lacks a critical and comparative view of the sources, even to ones that were accessible to him and that he cites.

It would be risky to attempt to understand the Modern Greek folk beliefs and traditions and their relation to antiquity based entirely on Lawson's study. Though its value is still today unquestionable, and after a century it may be a point of reference and a valuable source of ethnographic data, we must not forget about the time it was written and about the general, stereotypical view of the intellectuals concerning the existence of Modern Greece in West European thought.[331] How could they have comprehended the place where Nymphs are still dancing with the satyrs and the Angels help ancient Greek Charon, whom the Almighty ordered to take up disagreeable duties and lead all the souls to the somber Hades…?

3. Charos *nekropompos*

Among different representations of Charos, one is especially worth closer examination, as it brings to mind reminiscences of older convictions and beliefs, supposedly of ancient origin, connected with the eschatological sphere of Charos' activity. These are some motives of the Modern Greek folks songs containing the scene of leading the dead by Charos, who in such cases could be regarded as the modern counterpart of the ancient Hermes. Yet, as the ancient Greek Hermes led the souls (psychai) to Hades and consequently gained the name of *psychopompos*, modern Charos from demotic songs leads the deceased, not their souls. Considering this, the question arises as to if Charos retains any features of his ancient predecessor and indeed plays his role,[332] or if the folk im-

---

time, he did not attempt to trace and research the practices of the intervening periods from the conversion to Christianity until the end of the Ottoman Empire. See Hartnup 2004: 8.

331 See the chapter "Sources."

332 Lawson, based on Abbot's research, mentions that in some districts of Macedonia, Thrace and Asia Minor an ancient custom of placing a small coin in the mouth of the dead prevailed, but it was remembered at that time only by some old locals. Abbot 1903; Lawson 1910: 108 f. See Bzinkowski 2009: 29.

agination created such a picture under any foreign influence. I shall concentrate in the next part of this book on two motives connected with Charos leading the dead, trying to shed some light on the question of the possible origins of such an image and the context.

The procession of Charos

One of the most popular motives related to Charos, widespread throughout Greece and known in countless versions, could be called "the procession of Charos" or "Charos leading the dead."[333] Due to the abundance of comparative material, it is obviously not possible to gather all the existing variants and pay attention to all their peculiarities. I shall only present the most typical ones, trying to catch their most characteristic features.

In the first verse of the songs containing this motif, usually a seemingly rhetorical question appears that introduces the coming of Charos, preparing in a way the stage for his appearance. The attention is focused on strange natural phenomena, such as the mountains unexpectedly turning black or foggy, assuming a look as if they had just started to lament and prepared for the passage of Charos. All the nature seems to function as a harbinger of the approaching Death-Charos.[334] The introductory verse might be realized by use of different forms of expression, nevertheless it remains the same as for the mood and image:

> Τι είναι μαύρα τα βουνά, και στέκουν βουρκωμένα; (Saunier 5α, p. 382; Kriaris p. 327)[335]
> *Why are the mountains black and they stand foggy?*
>
> Αναστενάζουν τα βουνά κι οι κάμποι αγλογάνε! (Sklaventis 37)
> *The mountains sigh and the fields weep!*
>
> Το βλέπεις κείνο το βουνό, που 'ναι καψαλισμένο; (EDT, 131)
> *Do you see that mountain that is burnt?*

---

[333] Saunier enumerates among others: Peloponnesus, Central Greece, Epirus, the Heptanese, west Macedonia, Thrace, Milos, Nisiros, Crete, Pontus. Saunier 1999: 383.

[334] Hutter, Sikke 1979: 62.

[335] Saunier cites Fauriel's version (II, 228) noting that Politis' version (218) is undoubtedly artificial due to many words not belonging to demotic Greek. Saunier 1999: 383.

Το βλέπεις 'κείνο το βουνό, πούναι τσουλαβρισμένο; (Kougeas 65)
Do you see that mountain that is scorched?

Το βλέπεις κείνο το βουνό, που είν' πιο ψηλό από τ' άλλα; (Matsinopoulos Δ-12, β')
Do you see that mountain that is higher than others?

Πολλή μαυρίλα στα βουνά και κατσαχνιά μεγάλη. (Pasayanis 30)
A lot of blackness in the mountains, dense fog.

Γιατί είναι μαύρα τα βουνά, γιατ' είναι ανταριασμένα; (Kondomichis 3, p. 171)[336]
Why are the mountains black, why are they turbulent?

The continuous questions, if it is the wind or the rain causing such a gloomy image, and the following negative answers lead to the simple statement underlining the natural – as it seems – cause of things, namely the passage of Charos with the dead:

μόνε διαβαίν' ο Χάροντας με τους αποθαμένους. (Saunier 5α, p. 382; Matsinopoulos Δ-11, α')
Only Charondas passes with the dead.

Εκεί έχει ο Χάρος πέρασμα, περνάει τους πεθαμένους (Matsinopoulos Δ-12, α', β')
There Charos passes, he leads the dead.

In most versions, the next lines include the well-known image of the procession of Charos, who leads (dragging or just taking) the young men (τους νεούς) in front of him, the old ones (τους γέροντας) behind, whereas the children (τα μικρά παιδιά, τα παιδόπουλα) hang on the saddle.

Σέρνει τους νεούς από μπροστά, τους γέροντες κατόπι,
τα τρυφερά παιδόπουλα στη σέλλ' αραδιασμένα. (Saunier 5α, p. 382. Almost identical versions see Motsios 56; Kapsalis 653; Ioannou 275; Kondomichis 3, p. 171)
He drags the young in front, the old behind,
he has the fragile children arrayed to the saddle.

---

[336] Interestingly, this is not the first verse of the song. It is preceded by a rhymed distich: Σήμερα μαύρος ουρανός, σήμερα μαύρη μέρα/ σήμερα ξεχωρίζουνε αϊτός και περιστέρα. (*Today the sky is black, today the day is black/ today the eagle and the dove distinguish.*)

In some versions, there are also other groups of his "entourage" that seem to consist of different social groups: housewives (νοικοκυρές), ploughmen (ζευγολάτες), lords (άρχοντας), officers (αξιωματικούς):

φέρνει και τις νοικοκυρές ψηλά ανασκουμπωμένες,
φέρνει και τους ζευγολάτες με τα σκοινιά στον ώμο. (EDT 131)
He carries the housewives that are gathered highly,
he carries the ploughmen with the ropes on their arms.

σούρνει τους άρχοντας φλομούς, τη φτώχεια μαραμένη,
σούρνει και τα μικρά παιδιά στ' αλόγου τη σέλα. (Kougeas 65)
He drags the pale lords, the poor withered,
he drags little children at the saddle.

Μα είχε τους άρχοντες μπροστά και τους φτωχούς ξοπίσω,
κι είχ' απ' τους αξιωματικούς βγαλμένα τα γαλόνια,
είχε και τα μικρά παιδιά στη σκάλα τ' άλογού του. (Pasayanis 26)
He had the lords in front, the poor behind,
he had the stripes taken off the officers,
he had little children at the stirrup of his horse.

In different versions, we come cross the same oral formula, but slightly changed by incorporating the element we have already seen in the *charopalema* motif of "pulling the hair"[337]:

Σέρνει τους νιους απ' τα μαλλιά, τους γέρους απ' τα χέρια.[338]
πιάνει το νιο' που τα μαλλιά, χάμαις τον γονατίζει. (Politis 215)
He drags the young by the hair, the old by the hands,
he catches a young boy by his hair, he makes him kneel.

Παίρνει τους νιους απ' τα μαλλιά, τους γέρους απ' τα χέρια,
παίρνει και τα μικρά παιδιά ανάμεσα στη σέλα. (Motsios 246; see also Sklavenitis 37)
He takes the young by the hair, the old by the hand,
he takes little children in the middle of his saddle.

The subsequent parts of the song, regardless of the variant, are rather uniform and don't vary in the most important details. The dead ask Cha-

---

[337] Omatos 1990: 309 makes an interesting suggestion that the motif of pulling the hair recalls ancient sacrificial rites starting with the cutting of the hair of a victim. She also recalls the custom of putting strands of hair on tombs as an offering to the dead. She makes a reference to Eurypides' *Alkestis* (98 ff.) where the hair was hung on the door of the deceased. Pulling the hair might also be understood as taking the physical powers. Hutter, Sikke 1979: 64.

[338] Cited by Omatos 1990: 309.

ros to pass through villages so that they could see their relatives but he refuses, arguing that – significantly – it might cause unbearable grief for the living and they would recognize and try to embrace the dead, and it would be too difficult to part with them. Consequently, the procession of Charos disappears, which however is not explicitly expressed. We will not find anywhere, in any version – at least I have not found such – the information often repeated by commentators,[339] that Charos leads the dead to Hades. Yet, both the image as well as the frequency of its occurrence in demotic songs may prove that he seems to function as someone introducing the deceased to the other stage of existence.[340]

It has been suggested that the origins of the representation of the procession of Charos might be sought in acritic songs,[341] however, such an assumption was not supported by any convincing evidence. It seems as if the motif of "pulling the hair," relatively rare in "the procession of Charos" but appearing in the *charopalema* cycle,[342] or the mention of Charos' black horse, might have projected on the associations of the researchers and brought about such a hypothesis.

The subsequent example of the version of the analysed motif may be a good illustration, as I suppose, for extending the research into the context of the possible sources of inspiration regarding such a representation. There is an extremely rare type of song in which a figure similar to Charos, although it is not expressed explicitly, is called Αντρειόβλαχος, which could be translated as "The Brave Vlach." He drags nine brothers chained together, similarly as if Charos led the dead.

> Σέρνει ο Αντρειόβλαχος εννιά αδερφούς δεμένους
> σε μιαν άλυσο, σε μια μακρειά αλυσίδα.
> Πάει κ' η μάννα τους, κοντά περικαλιώντα:
> 'Φέντη Αντρειόβλαχε, αφέντη των παιδιών μου,
> χάρισε κ' εμέ κανέν' απ' τα παιδιά μου
> το μικρότερο, το μεγαλύτερο μου'. (Politis 210)[343]
> *The Brave Vlach drags nine brothers bound*
> *in one chain, in one long chain.*

---

[339] Anagnostopoulos 1984: 88–89.

[340] Hutter, Sikke 1979: 61.

[341] Kougeas 2000: 62; Sklavenitis 2012: 83.

[342] See the chapter "Wrestling or playing with Charos".

[343] There is a similar version in Saunier (9γ, p. 392), where instead of αφέντη των παιδιών μου, we have: πατέρα των παιδιώ μου.

Their mother comes closer, begging:
'Dear Lord, the Brave Vlach, lord of my children,
give me any one of my children
the youngest one, the oldest one.'

Saunier himself, who includes this song into the category of songs he calls collectively "Charos," admits he does not know where such a name of Charos might come from.[344] This may seem weird if we remember his tendency to link most of the representations of Charos with historical events. In my opinion, the problem is different, the question is whether this very song really alludes to Charos.

Spiridakis, who found nineteen versions of this song, most of them with the name Τάταρης or Ταρτάρης, convincingly proves that this song was mistakenly associated thematically with the figure of Charos. According to him, Nikolaos Politis, who published the above-mentioned song in his well-known collection (1914), made a compilation of two existing variants.[345] Politis himself commented on the name of "The Brave Vlach," deciding ex cathedra that Αντρειόβλαχος as well as in other versions, "Tataris," is no other than Charos and classified this song as *miroloi* because of its allegorical, according to his opinion, content. Spiridakis goes on and explains that the name "Tataris" has no connection at all with Tartaris – the other name of Charos we sporadically find[346] – and alludes to the Turkish word *tatar*, namely to a mounted messenger of the Sultan during the turkokratia.[347] Thus, according to him, this is without any doubt not a lament song about Charos, but it reflects the memory of the Sultan's orders to imprison some persons

---

[344] Saunier 1999: 393.

[345] Spiridakis 1956: 45 ff. He thoroughly analyses all the variants paying attention not only to the differences as to the misunderstanding in interpreting it as a lament song.

[346] A version, in which instead of "The Brave Vlach" appears Tartaris (Τάρταρης), is found in Saunier: σέρνει ο Τάρταρης [...] – Αφέντη Τάρταρη, κι αφέντη των παδιών μου. (Saunier 9α, p. 390). Interestingly, in another version in Saunier with the name Tartaris we find an enigmatic phrase: – Σκύλε Τάρταρη, Χάροντα των παιδιών μου. (Saunier 9β, p. 392) We find the same phrase in Kriaris (p. 310, entitled significantly: Παράκλησις προς τον Τάρταρη Χάροντα). I think in both cases the name Charos might be understood rather as a casual synonym to death and its personification.

[347] We come across the name Tataris in many Greek folk songs. Spiridakis 1956: 47 ff.

dangerous for the state.[348] As a matter of fact, the nine brothers from the above-mentioned song could be a distant reflection of children being taken away from their mothers, not an allusion to dead brothers,[349] as it was misunderstood. I share his opinion, yet I wonder, why he – as the other ones – omitted any attempt to explain the name Αντρειόβλαχος.

Even if we assume, as it has been suggested elsewhere, that the name is just another version of the name Andronikos[350] that we come across in acritic songs, or that the whole song is just a reflection of prisoners taken during the turkokratia, we still don't solve the puzzle as to why one name is replaced by another one, which is rather odd at first sight. Thus, maybe the explanation lies somewhere else.

Undoubtedly, one could easily associate the name of Charos from the cited song with the ethnic group called Vlachs[351] living mainly in northern parts of Greece. For centuries, they have coexisted with the Greeks, introducing some elements from their traditional culture into the folklore of Modern Greece and, of course, borrowing some elements from them. The question that arises is why Charos could in any way be identified with a Vlach…? I would not say it is a derisive way of calling him, since in the cited version the situational context is rather serious: a desperate mother who begs Charos/The Vlach to give her back at least her youngest son. Moreover, the places in which Politis registered the songs are not situated in the parts of Greece inhabited by Vlachs, but in Lakonia and Arcadia. Is this just another resonance of any historical memory of the Vlachs and the fear they might have caused during their sudden appearance in the mountainous villages? The question remains open and would be worth further research, I suppose.

---

[348] Spiridakis 1956: 46 ff.

[349] Spiridakis (1956: 51) makes a suggestion that a well-known ballad about nine dead brothers from Cappadocia might have been the main source of inspiration for the subsequent versions about Tataris.

[350] Romaios 1979: 235–236.

[351] In Greek they are called *Armanoi/Aromouni* (Αρμάνοι/Αρωμούνοι) or *Vlachoi* (Βλάχοι).

The ship of the dead

In the folklore of Modern Greece there are no evident and doubtless traces of Charos as a ferryman carrying the souls across the river or the lake.[352] Yet, another intriguing representation of Charos that we sporadically come across in songs from different part of Greece,[353] especially from the Mani Peninsula and some islands, is integrally connected with the motif of the ship of the dead.

The figure of a ship carrying the dead or the souls may, of course, convey the most archaic concepts of the passage to the Underworld.[354] However, it seems to me, which I shall attempt to show, that in this case this apparently mythological image might be explained in a different way, using different associations.

It is noteworthy that we come across such an image in the Modern Greek version that is very close to the well-known, in European nautical folk tradition, story of a ghost ship known as the Flying Dutchman.[355]

---

352 Anagnostopoulos 1984: 90. Bzinkowski 2009: 30. I have found only one extraordinary example linking Charos to a boat and thus seemingly associating him with ancient Charon. In Michailidis-Nouaros' collection of Karpathiaka, there is a very unusual song – repeated later in Makris' collection of Dodecanese songs (Makris 25, p. 257) where Charos surprisingly appears – not vividly but in an allusive way – as a boatman. The person speaking here asks Charos to bring him his boat so that he could go alone: Φέρε μου βάρκα, Χάροντα, κ' εγιώ 'μαι παλικαρι (*Bring me the boat, Charos, I am also a brave young man*, Michailidis-Nouaros, p. 139). There are two such songs from Zakynthos in Schmidt's collection (37, 38), but he himself has many doubts as to their genuineness. Dawkins 1942: 1939.

353 Songs about the ship of the dead are very rare, which may mean that the idea might have been rather borrowed from elsewhere, intertwined with local motives and incorporated in the corpus of demotic songs. For instance, we can not find any examples of this kind in EDT, nor in Politis, nor in Kougeas.

354 De Vries 1974: 420–421. Ships were used, among others, as a symbolic representation of the human body carrying the soul. Moreover, for Egyptians they were grave-gifts. German peoples used the shape of the ship as a grave or even the whole ships were buried with the body.

355 It is interesting to notice that the motif became very popular just at the beginning of the nineteenth century, namely the time the romantic movement urged forward the interest in folklore and stimulated the research on Modern Greek folklore. Apart from Coleridge's poem *The Rime of the Ancient Mariner* (1797–1798), there was Wagner's well-known opera *The Flying Dutchman* (1843) composed under Heine's influence who in his *Aus den Memoiren des Herrn von Schnabelewopski* (1833) mentions a theatrical

In the famous classification of Thomson, the whole story is concisely summarized as follows: "A sea captain, because of his wickedness sails his phantom ship eternally without coming to harbour."[356] Although not all elements of the description correspond to the Greek version, it seems it contains some common features, which I shall attempt to show below.

It may seem probable, although I realize it is not possible to be proved at all, that Modern Greek folk tradition, especially of the islands, knew a story of a ghost ship that was popular in West European folk tradition as early as the seventeenth century. As people of the sea, the Greeks had incessant contact with the other nations sailing to and fro and bringing goods, as well as their own stories transmitted in oral tradition by sea men. It would not be groundless to assume that those stories might have been interwoven in folk imagination with the local ones, creating a unique original account containing both older Greek elements and the inherited ones.

Generally, the plot of the Greek version of the ship of the dead follows, in most cases, the same scheme: a ghost ship approaches the land, the living run to see their dead relatives, but the ship disappears because of different reasons that vary according to the given variant. It is worth underlining that, although in some collections these songs are classified or entitled as *Charos' Ship* (*Του Χάρου το καράβι*, Pasayanis 102), there is no mention of the name of Charos at all. Thus, I would suppose these kinds of songs – due to their eschatological dimension and close similarity to the songs with a motif of procession with Charos – might have been unjustly associated with Charos by folklore researchers. In other words, calling Charos "the captain of the ship of the dead" as some researchers propose,[357] seems to be rather a misinterpretation and interpolation from elsewhere.

In the beginning, we usually come across a mention of the ship (το καράβι) that – according to different versions – may appear directly at sea:

---

performance of *The Flying Dutchman* in Amsterdam, as well as the novel *The Phantom Ship* (1839) by Frederick Marryat. Janion 1987: 11–16.

[356] Thompson 1955–1958: E511.

[357] Anagnostopoulos 1984: 90.

Ένα καράβι στο γιαλό λεβέντες φορτωμένο. (Pasayanis 43, p. 24; Petropoulos 81 A'; Saunier 8α, p. 208)
A ship at sea loaded with brave young men.

Ένα καράβι αγνάντεψα λεβέντες φορτωμένο. (Kondomichis 58, Lefkada)
I discerned a ship at sea loaded with brave young men.

Καράβι νεξαγνάντισε στη μέση του πελάγου. (Pasayanis 102)
He discerned in the middle of the sea a ship.

Instead of a simple "ship," in some versions "a steamship" appears (το βαπόρι):

Αντίκρια στο Βενετικό έρχεται ένα παπόρι. (Kougeas 54)
Opposite the Ventiko island a ship is sailing.

Interestingly, in the versions from the Mani Peninsula, another kind of ship is mentioned, namely a galley (το κάτεργο). Moreover, in this case we come across three ships:

Τρία κάτεργα αγναντέψανε στη μέση του πελάγους. (Kougeas 81; 123)
Three galleys appeared in the middle of the sea.

Αγνάντια στο Βενέτικο τρία κάτεργα αγνάντεψαν. (Kougeas 52)
Opposite the Ventiko island three galleys appeared.

Αντίκρυ απ' το Βενέτικο έρχονται τρία καράβια. (Pasayanis 40)
From the opposite side, from the Ventiko island, three ships are coming.

Or, in rare cases, it comes directly from the earth and the lower world:

Καράβι βγαίνει από τη γη, κι από τον κάτου κόσμο. (Petropoulos 81 B'; Saunier 8β, p. 208)
A ship is coming out from the earth, from the Underworld.

The second feature that is repeated in all versions of the story is a division of the dead accordingly to the place on the ship. The explicit formulaic composition of the first lines of different versions brings analogies to the picture of the procession of Charos that I have already alluded to.

Thus, in some cases, we have three or four sorts of dead, regardless of the part of the ship, which are interchangeable in different variants in Kougeas' collection:

politicians, mayors	πολιτικοί, δήμαρχοι (Kougeas 72)
slim girls	λυγερές (Kougeas 52; 54; 81)

brave boys	λεβέντες (Kougeas 52; 54; 81; 123), λεβεντουργιά (Kougeas 72)
hosts	νοικοκυραίοι, οικοδεσπότες (Kougeas 52; 54)
small children	μικρά παιδιά (Kougeas 72; 54; 81; 101)
priests	παπάδες (Kougeas 88)
the brave	αντρειωμένοι (Kougeas 101)
lords	άρχοντες (Kougeas 101)
old men	γέροντες (Kougeas 123)

Interestingly, in Saunier's and Pasayanis' collections, slightly different groups appear:

> (ill) άρρωστοι, (wounded) λαβωμένοι, (drowned at the sea) θαλασσοπνιγμένοι (Saunier 8α, p. 208, Laconia – apparently drawn from Pasayanis 43, Kondomichis 58, p. 159)
> (old men) γέροντες, (young boys) παλληκάρια, (small children) μικρά παιδάκια (Saunier 8β, p. 208, Trifylia)
> (old men) γέροντες, (young boys) παλικάρια, (young girls) κορασίδες (Pasayanis 40)

If we compare the categories of the passengers of the ghost ship in Kougeas and the other two collections, we notice that the former are more specific, including some defined social groups, yet the latter allude only generally to people according to their age. It is noteworthy that Kougeas himself thought that the people mentioned above, especially in Song 72, might be a reflection of a real historical event during which a ship transporting some significant people sank after the captain's manoeuvre.[358] Thus, the other versions, according to him, could be regarded as derivatives of 72. Simultaneously, he pays attention to the fact that it is not possible to trace exactly the historical source of the song.[359] I would disagree with such a statement and would rather suggest it might have been adversely. As I suppose, there might have been some songs of this kind in oral tradition, regardless of their origin, which is partly confirmed as we also come across them in other parts of Greece (Ithaca, Lakonia), not exclusively in Mani. Secondly, if Song 72 could be a source of other ones about the ship of the dead, there is a high probability that some of them could be preserved and noted in collections of folks songs, which, as far as I know, did not happen. Instead,

358 Kougeas 2000: 85–86.

359 Kougeas 2000: 85.

we have only one such existing version – at least I have not found any other similar ones – which differs a lot from the other ones of this kind. Song 72 gives some real topographical features: the ship is coming from Chios. Interestingly, in other versions in Kougeas, the action takes place close to a small island called Venetiko, which, in fact, is situated in the south-eastern part of Chios, but an island with such a name also exists in the Messenian Gulf close to Mani.[360] The problem of geographical names in Greek ballads and folk songs is clearly visible in the example of the mythical Bridge of Arta, which, of course, does not allude to the real bridge in Greece, but is just an existing topographical equivalent of a mythical, symbolical place of passage.[361] The same situation, but naturally not necessarily, as it seems to me, might have happened with the Venetico island. I am convinced here that we are dealing with the language of eschatological imagery, expressing the moment of passage to the other world. Thus, it seems more natural that the passengers of the ship would be described rather in general terms than regarding their social position, like in Song 72.

The rest of the story about the ghost ship follows a scheme that slightly differs according to peculiar variants. In most cases, there is a rumour in the neighbouring villages that the ship with their dead relatives is coming closer, widows, mothers and sisters run and gather to greet their relatives, but the ship (or ships) vanishes (Kougeas 52; Pasayanis 43) or sinks (Kougeas 123).[362] In some cases, the passengers themselves ask the captain, who is not named, to get closer so that they could visit their living relatives, but the captain refuses.

A different variant is recorded in a version cited by Saunier, where the dead themselves ask Charos not to land (Saunier 12, p. 400), which is a very rare example where Charos himself appears.[363] However, in this very case we come across a variant differing completely in comparison with the ones cited above. Charos in this song is a builder – the role

---

[360] Kougeas 2000: 85.

[361] Beaton 2004: 120–124.

[362] In some cases, the narrator of the story begs the captain to sail to Kitres (Kougeas 52) or the dead themselves ask him not to approach the villages in order not to bring about more grief and lament.

[363] Saunier 1999: 401.

I shall outline in the following chapter – but instead of a tower or a castle – he builds a steamship:

> Του Χάρου το βουλήθηκε παπόρι να σκαριώσει. (Saunier 12, p. 400, Ithaca)[364]
> *Charos wanted to build a steamship.*

The difference between this song and the other ones with the motif of a ship lies in the role the dead play. Whereas in the previous fragments they were just passengers, here they constitute the parts of the ship, as following: γέροι – σκαριά (the old – hulls), νιοι – μαδέρια (the young – wooden planks), παλικάρια – αντενοκάταρτα (the young brave – masts), ξανθομαλλών πλεξίδες – ξάρτια (braids of the blonde-haired girls – shrouds), μικρών παιδιών κουφούλες, μικρών παιδιών κεφάλια – πανιά, μικρω̃ν παιδιών κεφάλια – αντενοκάρουλα (small children's heads – the sails/ the crow's nests).

The composition of this song shows the strong influence of the motif of Charos the builder and seems to be yet another version of the songs belonging to that type.

The rarity of such representations of Charos indicate that his connection with the sea is rather limited, his area of activity is exclusively the land, the Greek mainland, he seems not to have any connections with water and the songs containing this element might have been created *per analogiam* to other songs.

The question that arises is, why for the Greeks, for whom the sea is always in folk tradition regarded as "bitter" (θάλασσα, πικροθάλασσα και πικροκυματούσα, EDT 155 – *The sea, the bitter sea, bitterly undulant*), the sea that takes forever their relatives – where they die or they just go abroad to foreign lands – has it almost no connection with the personified Death in Charos' mask? Scant evidence found in Greek folk songs prove that Death and the sea are something unusual in the folk eschatology of the Modern Greeks. It is symptomatic, because one can have the impression that it is not the sea that is the most dangerous place whence Death may come, but the land. Indeed, as I have already demonstrated, even the representation of Charos as a pirate is not as frequent as it could be, if we take into account the historical reasons sug-

---

364 We come across a different variant in Sklavenitis 2012: 68 (cited from Giofyllis, Thiaka p. 99, 2).

gested by Saunier,[365] but as it seems, also in this kind of representation, emphasis is put rather on his destroying activity.

Summarizing the deliberations about the motif of the ship of the dead and its connection with Charos, let me underline that the rare frequency of such a representation rather suggests a foreign source of inspiration. If we juxtapose the above-mentioned songs with the Flying Dutchman story that I have alluded to, we could see some common features, although, of course, many more differences. However, the image of a ship where the passengers are the dead and a recurring motif of approaching the coast and then disappearing may suggest that the Modern Greek versions may have something in common with the folk story known to West Europeans.

Yet, even if we could perceive the figure of a ghost ship from Modern Greek songs as a symbolic representation of a passage to the other world, the motif recurring in all ancient mythologies with the usage of a boat imagery,[366] some difficulties arise. First of all, the ship does not travel to the Netherworld or elsewhere, but strays away – similarly to the Flying Dutchman. Secondly, except one song with a motif of Charos building a steamship, there is no ferryman or any *nekropompos* that we could associate with the passage to the other world and thus link it to the mythological representations.

It seems that, in this case, we are dealing rather with a conflation of the story about a ghost ship, popular in European folk tradition, with the motif of the procession of Charos we come across in different part of Greece.

---

[365] Saunier recalls that in "The Chronicle of Galaxeidi" (Χρονικό του Γαλαξειδίου) written in 1703 by the monk Euthymios in the vernacular language, the word κουρσάροι is used mainly for Bulgar occupants in the tenth century as well as the pirates of Roger II of Sicily. Saunier 1982, 305.

[366] There are some examples of identifying the dead with a boat in Greek folk songs. See, for example: Pasayanis (καράβι μου τρικάταρτο… Pasayanis 19; 52; Saunier 5δ, 268; Sklavenitis 55, φρεγάδα μου τρικάταρτη… (Sklavenitis 56), καράβι πρωτοτάξιδο… Pasayanis 90; Saunier 15γ, 92, Kalamata) with the apostrophes to the dead using the metaphor of a ship. See also different variants in Sklavenitis 2012: 100–102.

4. Charos the builder

One of the most intriguing representations of Charos is connected with his activity as a builder of different kinds of things, most often a tower or a garden. However, he does not use common building materials in his works, but the bodies of the dead. The motif of building a tower (πύργος) is known mainly on the Ionian Islands, in Peloponnesus and in the region of Aetolia-Acarnania, but there is also a variant from Cappadocia.[367] In turn, we come across the garden or the orchard (περιβόλι, μπαξές) motif in Peloponnesus, especially in Lakonia, the Mani Peninsula and Messenia, as well as in Crete, the Ionian Islands, the Aegean Islands, but also in Cappadocia.[368] Apart from these two motives, which are undoubtedly the most frequent and, at the same time, relatively homogenized, here and there we could also find some untypical representations of Charos building a palace (παλάτι), houses (σπίτια), a factory (φάμπρικα), jails (φυλακές) or even a monastery (μοναστήρι). I shall try to elucidate the context of such a macabre image, also shedding some light on possible sources as well as unsuccessful, so far, attempts to interpret the motif.

In most cases, the beginning of a song has an introductory formula specifying the construction Charos is going to build. In the following example, it is a tower:

> Του Χάρου του βουλήθηκε πύργο να θεμελιώσει. (Saunier 10α, p. 392; 10β, 10γ, 10δ, p. 394; Kougeas 79; 3; 69; Pasayanis 8; 102)
> *Charos wanted to erect a tower.*

Two elements appear invariably as a permanent component and they seem to be always linked to the same category of the dead: foundation (θέμελο) – the old men (γέροι), cornerstone (αγκωνάρι) – the young (νέοι).

The third element, children, is variable. It may also be: windows (παραθύρια, Saunier 10α, p. 392), battlements (μεντένια, Saunier 10β,

[367] Saunier 1999: 395. Dawkins pays attention to the fact that the motif of tower is better understood in Mani, where almost every house has a real tower built as a shelter or a place of defence in case of vendetta. Dawkins 1942: 138–139.

[368] Saunier 1999: 397.

p. 394), small stones in the walls (σόμπολα, Saunier 10γ, 10δ, p. 394), wooden nails in windows (τσιβιά, Saunier 10ε, p. 394), or pebbles (μικρούλια χαλικάκια, Kougeas 79). The most macabre image emerges when children are called to be soil itself (χώματα, Kougeas 69).

In some cases, three components are not enough and the framework of the image is extended by introducing some other categories of the dead juxtaposed with the parts of a building. As the rafters (μετζανόξυλα) and the floor (πατωμάτερα) Charos uses the arms of young men (παλληκαριώνε μπράτζα, Saunier 10γ, 10δ, p. 394). In place of doors and windows (πορτοπαράθυρα) he puts good landladies (καλές νοικοκουράδες, Saunier 10γ, p. 394; Kougeas 3) or just young girls (Kougeas 79). The roof battens (σταλίκια) are built of girls' braids (κορασιδών πλεξίδες, Saunier 10δ, p. 394).

All the untypical variants of the tower motif, although introduced by the different kinds of construction Charos is going to build (house, factory, monastery), follow almost the same pattern regarding the juxtaposition of the dead and building material. Only the introductory formulas vary:

Ο Χάρος έβαλε βουλή να χτίσει ένα παλάτι. (Saunier 10ε, p. 394)
Charos decided to build a palace.

Ο Χάρος σπίτια έφτιανε κι ο Χάρος σπίτια χτίζει. (Kapsalis 645)
Charos built houses, Charos builds houses.

Ο Χάρος φκιάνει φάμπρικα, φκιάνει καινούρια σπίτια. (Kondomichis 20, p. 176, Lefkada)
Charos builds a factory, he builds new houses.

Ο Χάρος έβαλε βουλή να χτίσει μοναστήρι.[369]
Charos decided to build a monastery.

Here are some examples with an extended introduction:

Ο Χάρος εκατέβηκε από τον κάτω κόσμο,
παίρνει ανθρώπους για δουλειά, θέλει να χτίσει σπίτι. (Kondomichis 7, p. 172, Lefkada)
Charos emerges from the Underworld,
he takes people to work, he wants to build a house.

---

369 According to Vangellio Vrettou, 75 years old, Charadiatika, Lefkada. Cited by Sklavenitis 2012: 67.

Κάτου στις πέτρινες αυλές, στα μαρμαρένια αλώνια,
ο Χάρος φκιάνει φάμπρικες και οικοδομές μεγάλες. (Sklavenitis 23)
Down at the stony courts, down at the marble threshing-floors,
Charos builds factories and huge buildings.

Similarly to this case, we have almost the same pairs as in the tower motif, with some unusual variants and occasionally, which is worth underlining, the elements are inverted. Thus, the foundation (θέμελο) is built not by the old ones as it was, but by the young, the cornerstone (αγκωνάρι) by the old ones (Kondomichis 7; 20; Sklavenitis 23; Sklavenitis 2012: 67). In Kapsalis' version from Northern Epirus we come across men (άντρες) as δέματα (probably here not just "parcels" but rather "links"), women as doors (πόρτες) and children as windows (παραθύρια, Kapsalis 645). In other versions, children are used as pebbles (χαλίκι, Kondomichis 20), or large pebbles (τρόχαλα, Sklavenitis 23). There are also women – good housewives (καλές νοικοκυρές, Kondomichis 7) used by Charos as windows and girls as doors (πορτοπούλες, Sklavenitis 2012: 67).

It is noteworthy that in these cases there is no category of old men who would compose any kind of enclosure of the construction.

The garden or orchard motif is similarly introduced by a formula "Charos wanted/decided to build/plant a garden" that appears rather invariable with insignificant changes[370]:

Ο Χάρος εβουλήθηκε να φτιάσει περιβόλι. (Saunier 11α, 11β, 11γ, p. 396; Kougeas 75; 14; 6; 114; Pasayanis 7; 9)
Charos wanted to plant a garden.

Ο Χάρος τ' αποφάσισε να φκιάσει περιβόλι. (Kondomichis 21, p. 176; Kougeas 138)
Charos decided to plant a garden.

Όταν εχτίστη ο Ουρανός κι εθεμελιώθη ο κόσμος
Ο Χάρος τότε αρχίνησε να φτιάνει περιβόλι. (Pasayanis 10)
When The Heavens were built and the world was founded
then Charos started to plant a garden.

---

370 Borowska 2011: 132.

There is also an interesting version from Passow, mentioned by Saunier[371] and repeated by Stathis,[372] in which Charos invites people to build the garden with him and the ones who help will be freed by him. In this variant Charos "trumpeted" (διαλάλησε) he is going to plant a garden:

> Ο Χάρος εδιαλάλησε να κτίσει περιβόλι,
> όποιος βρεθεί και κτίσει το να τον ελευθερώσει. (Passow 435)
> *Charos announced he wanted to build a garden,*
> *and whoever will come and build, he will let him out.*

In the garden or the orchard, the dead in most versions are associated with the following kinds of trees: young girls (νιες) – lemon trees (λεμόνια), young boys (νιοι) – cypresses (κυπαρίσσια). As for children (παιδιά), they are linked to different kinds of plants. They become either roses (τριαντάφυλλα, Saunier 11α, p. 396), or mint and carnations (δύασμοι και καρυοφύλλια, Saunier 11β, p. 396), or carnations and violets (γαρούφαλλα και βιόλες, Saunier 11γ, p. 396; Kougeas 138; 6; 14), or just flowers (ανθοί, Kondomichis 21).

What is significant in the description of Charos' garden is the complete lack of the category of old men, which was an integral part of the tower he built. It might, of course, be explained by the imagery of the vegetation cycle and the spring rebirth of the plants that leaves no space for old age. Yet such an assumption may be seemingly misleading, it turns out that there are many variants of the motif of Charos' garden in which the category of old men (γέροντες) appears. However, their place is not among the plants, they invariably become the fence or the wall of the garden (φράχτη, τοίχος, Pasayanis 7; 10; Kougeas 138; 14) or just fence pales (πάσσαλοι, Kondomichis 21).

In some versions, the description of the garden is followed by the wish of a woman to die, step into this garden and cut down the plants

---

[371] In Saunier we come across an interesting variant taken from Passow (309: 435), in which young girls and boys do not constitute parts of the garden, but they run and gather to help him to build it. Saunier 11δ: 398. An untypical variant coming from Karpathos is noted also by Sklavenitis. Here Charos builds not only a garden but also jails (φυλακές). Sklavenitis 2012: 69. See also Manolakakis 95: Ο Χάρος χτίζει φυλακήν και κάμνει περιβόλι.

[372] Stathis 2004: 803.

(Saunier 11β, p. 396; Kougeas 75; 138) or just uproot the trees and the flowers and talk to the fence (Saunier 11γ, p. 396). In Schmidt's version from Zakynthos (Schmidt 164, p. 23), the woman comes to the garden to water the plants.[373]

* * *

Structurally, the tower and the garden motif, as we have seen, are almost identical. Both of them are introduced by a specific oral formula followed by juxtaposed enumeration of the dead used as a building material or the components of Charos' garden. The variability of the possible solutions within the framework of the structure of the motif is not significant. However, semantically both variants undoubtedly differ a lot from each other, a fact which is worth not only underlining but elaborating on.

In the case of Charos' tower, and by extension of all kinds of construction he builds in other variants of the motif, the emphasis of the image seems to stress an enclosure, a closed space being under the reign of Charos-Death. Although in some cases this enclosed area seems domesticated by the usage of the word "house" (σπίτι), it remains a dreary building composed of dead bodies. One could ask, as Saunier suggested elsewhere,[374] if the picture could be associated with another construction characteristic for Charos' domain, namely with a tent (τέντα), bringing to mind the military term, which I have already outlined above.

According to me, the tower motif in connection with Charos cannot be explained in these terms.[375] First of all, it is completely devoid of any other military elements and, as a matter of fact, is rather static, adversely to the above-mentioned image of Charos as an aggressor pulling the hair of his victims. Secondly, the similarity of the image postulated by Saunier to the representations of Hades that we could find in demotic

373 Saunier 1999: 397. We come across a similar motif in Kougeas' collection where a song appears that does not belong to the analysed motif but is rather a call for weeping and thus for watering by tears the garden of Charos. (Kougeas 13α). See also Borowska 2011: 132–133.

374 Saunier 1999: 364.

375 There is also no direct connection with acritic songs containing the motif of "garden of Digenis." Borowska 2011: 129.

songs is also groundless. If we take into account, for instance, the song 6γ, p. 238 with a description of the dead in the lower world, there are vivid discrepancies between the tower motif and that song, in which the dominating motif is "decomposition" and "decay" (Saunier 6γ, p. 238). In the analysed examples, all the bodies appear to be complete, the totality of the persons has not been touched, they are the whole as they were during their life, like the dead in the Homeric poems, but now they constitute a part of Charos' domain.

At this point, due to the many parallels that come into mind, I have to allude to the second variation of the motif of the dead being components of a construction. It has been suggested by Alexiou that Charos' garden belongs to the same imagery of plants and trees that is vital in popular tradition and is connected mainly with the images of spring and harvesting used – according to her – continuously in Greek tradition from antiquity until nowadays.[376] She argues that the idea of cutting the flowers, withering apples, falling leaves and especially of uprooted trees, occurring in countless examples in ancient Greek and later Byzantine literature, from the oldest lyric poets, through Homeric comparisons abounding in such images, also manifests itself in popular Modern Greek tradition.[377] And, of course, she is right in her suggestions, as I have already shown while analysing the figure of Charos as a reaper, she is no doubt right, at least partly.

In my opinion, the idea expressed in the songs where the figure of Charos the builder occurs has nothing in common either with military terms (in the case of the tower motif) or with spring and vegetation imagery (in the image of the garden of Charos), or – in no case – with the garden of Eden, as Stathis postulated.[378]

---

[376] Alexiou 2002: 195–201.

[377] Alexiou 2002: 195–201.

[378] Stathis 2004: 801. He believes that Charos' garden belongs to the same mythological tradition as Isles of the Blessed (μακάρων νῆσοι) or the Elysian Fields (Ἠλύσιον πεδίον) known from ancient Greek myths. Naturally, it is far from being possible due to the vivid discrepancy between the image the ancient prototypes convey and the modern folk version. However, Stathis further realizes that, in this case, this is "the most macabre garden in the world" and that rural Greek society imagined people in this garden not having the nature of the trees and flowers but being rather in their place. Stathis 2004: 803.

The most characteristic feature that – according to me – may be relevant in the songs analysed before, is the idea of the motionless, stillness, of the dead. All the groups constituting the components of the constructions may be characterized as passive and typical – without differentiating social status or introducing any individual elements. One could not get rid of the impression that, in the hands of Charos-Death, they become just elements of the landscape, integrally melted and fused with the surrounding reality. Charos, in turn, is not a violent aggressor here like he was in the representations outlined above, but rather a scrupulous worker. Significantly, the verbs that are used to describe his actions are totally neutral in meaning, not emphatic at all, as if he executed something typical for him: παίρνει – he takes, βάνει (βάζει) – he puts. In the garden motif, it is even more vivid: έσκαψε, καλλιέργησε, φύτεψε – he dug, cultivated, planted (Saunier 11α, p. 396) or έχτισε, καλλούργησε – he built, cultivated (Saunier 11γ, p. 396).

Such a picture is clearly different from the representation of Charos leading the procession of the dead, where he is depicted as a violent occupier, bringing to mind more his activity as a hunter or a reaper than a gardener. Although the motive of Charos leading the dead that I have presented in previous chapters is structurally similar and is constructed by the use of the oral formulas, it cannot by identified with Charos' activity as a builder. The whole scenery, according to me, with some typical kinds of trees, such as cypresses, and ephemeral flowers that constitute the elements of the landscape, inevitably brings to mind a picture of a cemetery. What may seem at first sight just a remote association grows in importance with a closer look. I don't say that the garden of Charos is a mythological representation of a cemetery. Yet, if we recall that the nineteenth century, at least in West Europe, was the beginning of a process when the dead ceased to be buried in graveyards and a new, independent place of burial, known and common today as a cemetery, was established,[379] the question becomes meaningful. Around 1800, the idea of a cemetery in the open nature, being a fragment of nature as well as creating a sort of a "small cosmos of death" surrounded by cypresses and separated from the world of the living, became increasingly popular.[380]

---

[379] Vovelle 2008: 540–545.

[380] Białostocki 2007: 123–125. Ariès 2011: 528–529.

Thus, maybe in folk imagination Charos-Death became in the course of time a gardener of the dead, in other words, the folk mythology was adapted to the changing reality and created such a unique picture of Death planting trees, flowers and herbs in the place enclosed by the fence of the old men, constituting a miniature of the kingdom of the dead. Or, it is just another mythical mask of the universal idea of cyclical time manifesting itself in the images both of decay and growth, dead bodies turning into soil and new flowers and trees growing from their ashes.

5. Charos' family

One of the most astonishing features of Charos, the element that clearly confirms that it would be an oversimplification to regard him just as a folk personification of death, is the fact that he has a family: his mother or wife, Charondissa/Charissa (Χαρόντισσα, Χάρισσα) or Charaina (Χάραινα) in the Pontus region and his children, Charopoula (Χαρόπουλα).

The role of Charissa is distinctly defined in songs where she is called his mother (μάνα), which I shall allude to below, however, in many cases she appears to be rather his wife, which is not explicitly expressed, and then her role is not so easily defined. In such cases, she appears in the company of their children or a child – Charopoulo (Χαρόπουλο). It is noteworthy that the motif of Charos' family is rather briefly sketched in Greek folk songs, it occurs now and then as an oral formula and in most cases is devoid of any special meaning.[381] As far as Charos' mother is concerned, it seems Charissa is significant and her appearance brings about a change and influences Charos' actions.

---

[381] In some cases, her name appears gnomically, like in a song from Leukada, where a dead man is speaking. He confesses that "he was invited by Charondissa for the feast" (Με κάλεσε η Χαρόντισσα τραπέζι να μου κάνει, Sklavenitis 3), which obviously metaphorically means that he died. She also appears in some formulaic expressions associated with the lower world: Κάτω στου Χάρου την αυλή, στης Χάραινας τις βρύσες (Saunier 7δ, p. 160), or: κρεμάει ο Χάρος το σπαθί κι η Χάρισσα τσεμπέρι (Ioannou 310).

The most frequently occurring pattern in the frame of this motif is a quarrel between Charos and his mother. Charondissa usually blames her son for bringing children who still need their mothers to the lower world, like in the song from Laconia that starts with the words of someone dead:

Όλον τον Άδη γύρισα με δυο κεριά αναμμένα
κι άκουσα τη Χαρόντισσα, που μάλωνε το Χάρο
– Χάρε, και τι μου το' φερες το πολυχαϊδεμένο; (Pasayanis 59; Saunier 2α, p. 372)
I walked the whole of Hades with two candles lit
and I heard Charondissa quarrelling with Charos
– Charos, why did you bring me here the one that was caressed so much?

The same motif appears in different versions and its main aim seems to contrast Charos and his mother, underlining the clemency of the latter.[382] She reproaches him for taking to Hades children that all the time cry and cannot be easily hushed (Saunier 2β, 2γ, p. 374; Saunier 20, p. 412; Ioannou 289; Pasayanis 59; Petropoluos 38 Ε', p. 234), or they don't want to eat (Ioannou 288), or that could rejoice the world instead of being here (Motsios 325). She blames Charos for taking young girls, in some cases newly-married, and young boys and those who have little children (Matsinopoulos Δ-14, α', β', γ', δ').

The figure of Charondissa as Charos' mother is also helpful for the living. One of the most widespread motives underlines her concern for people, especially for women. She warns mothers to hide their children and sisters to conceal their brothers from her cruel and merciless son.[383] Mostly, the motif is introduced by an oral formula according to the same structural pattern "Charos' mother shouted/spoke (διαλάλησε, χούγιαξεν, ρόαξε) from the high mountain top/window" (από ψηλή ραχούλα, απ' ώριο παραθύρι, Saunier 6β, p. 384; Saunier 6γ, p. 384; Kougeas 22α'; 127; 133; Pasayanis 21) with some slightly different variants:

Του Χάρου η μάνα τό λεγε στης εκκλησιάς την πόρτα. (Pasayanis 33; Matsinopoulos Δ-13, β')
Charos' mother spoke this in the door of the church.

---

382 Hutter, Sikke 1979: 61. Borowska 2008: 81. Charondissa's reaction is in some cases contrasted to those of Charos, while he laughs, she weeps, for instance: Το βλέπει ο Χάρος και γελά κι η Χάρισσα και κλαίει (Kondomichis 62).

383 Anagnostopoulos 1984: 93–94.

Του Χάρου η μάνα τό' λεγε, τό' λεγε μοιρολόγι. (Matsinopoulos Δ-13, α')
Charos' mother spoke this, she sang a lament song.

The scheme of her warning – sometimes explicitly expressed as her lament song (*miroloi*), like in the last example – is almost always the same and is also expressed in formulaic language. Charos appears in such cases mostly as a hunter (Kougeas 22α', 127; Saunier 6γ, p. 384; Pasayanis 21; Matsinopoulos Δ-13, β', γ'), which has already been demonstrated above, but also as a gardener (Kougeas 133) and a reaper (Saunier 6β, p. 384), or pirate and peddler (Saunier 6α, p. 384; Pasayanis 33; Matsinopoulos Δ-13, α') or just a passer-by who went for a walk (περατζάδα, Sklavenitis 14). The image of Charos that is revealed in his mother's words is rather threatening, among his characteristics his mercilessness is emphatically stressed.

For instance, in the following song, Charondissa orders other mothers to gather their children because the hunter is coming:

– Μαζώξτε, νιες, τους άντρες σας, μανάδες, τα παιδιά σας
τ' εβγήκε ο γυιος μου κυνηγός, δεν κυνηγάει αλάφια,
μόν' κυνηγάει νιους και νιες, πο' χουν μαύρα μάτια. (Saunier 6γ, p. 384)
– Gather, young ladies, your husbands, mothers, your children
my son went hunting, he doesn't hunt for deer,
only he hunts for young girls and boys, who have black eyes.

In Kougeas' collection there are similar versions of the hunting by Charos (Kougeas 22α, 127) and the motif of Charos' garden (Kougeas 133), however, the most interesting is a song that differs a lot from the other variants with Charos' mother. In this song, his mother appears to be a herald announcing a competition: the one who gets the wedding ring out of the well, as a reward will be enabled to go out of the lower world and come back to the world of the living, which naturally turns out to be impossible (Kougeas 26).

The name Charondissa in many cases, although it is not expressed directly, appears to be applied rather to Charos' wife. The context in which she is mentioned is connected mainly with the motif that we could call "Charos' dinner."[384] The person speaking here is someone dead who usually addresses his pleading to his mother so that she never

[384] Anagnostopoulos 1984: 95.

starts lamenting at the sunset, because at this time of the day Charos usually dines with his Charondissa (γιατί δειπνάει ο Χάροντας με την Χαρόντισσά του, Saunier 3γ, 3δ, p. 378; 3ε, p. 380; Stamatelos 7, p.19).[385] Most of the songs of such type are brief, however, there are some versions describing in detail the dinner in the Underworld. In one of them, noted in Ithaca, taken from Schmidt (166, 26) and cited in Saunier (3δ, p. 378), the scenery seems as if it comes from a completely different tradition, not the folk one, where such images do not appear almost at all in the eschatological context.

The vision of the plates upside-down (τα πιάτα ανάποδα), black table towels (τα τουβαλίθια μαύρα) and especially of "small children's heads" (μικρών παιδιών κεφάλια) on the table, and – instead of a dinner service – eagles' claws (σταυραϊτώνε χέρια)[386] as well as of the young as servants,[387] brings to mind rather grotesque paintings and sculptures. I do not mean here the medieval representations that were rather full of laughter, but the terrible Baroque images abounding in macabre figures.

The seventeenth-century iconography of death, especially in Italian and Spanish art, is focused on representing the idea of the passing of time and transience of human life. Thus, the paintings, alluding to medieval tradition, contain a lot of suggestive and realistically presented macabre elements, such as skulls, skeletons, cross-bones and other anatomical details. These features are clearly visible in seventeenth-century Baroque sepulchral sculpture. The purpose of all of these was to remind observers about the idea of *vanitas* of life.[388]

We come across such descriptions of the Underworld, alluding to this imagery and the macabre side of death, in the works composed in

---

[385] Cited by Sklavenitis 2012: 75.

[386] We find a similar image in Song 2δ cited by Saunier (p. 374) which also comes from Ithaca. Here, instead of "eagle claws" we have "the arms of the brave" (των αντρειωμένων μπράτσα). It is worth noting that in this song there is no mention of Charos but of his counterpart Mais (Μάης) and consequently of Maissa and Maiopoula (Μάϊσσα/Μαΐτσα, Μαγιόπουλα).

[387] Sometimes the dead complain that they had to serve at Charos' table. Dawkins 1942: 142.

[388] Białostocki 2007: 69–96. For more on the attitude of people of the Baroque towards death, see especially a monumental monograph by Vovelle 2008: 271ff. and Ariès 2011: 328–341.

Crete during the so-called "Cretan Renaissance," which I have alluded to several times.[389] The place of origin of two above-mentioned songs, one of the Ionian islands, suggests it is very probable the motif might have been borrowed directly from West European tradition.[390]

Another interesting example with macabre elements comes from Crete, another island under strong West European influence through the centuries. Moreover, this lament song, as Saunier comments, is exclusively Cretan.[391] In this song, according to the person speaking, who describes himself as "staying overnight in Charos' neighbourhood" (στου Χάροντα τη γειτονιά ήμουνε ξωμενάρης, Saunier 17, p. 406), Charos came back to Charondissa and told her he felt the "human's smell" (ανθρώπου μυρωδιά). His wife's answer reveals the reason for that smell, which comes from Charos himself, because "he comes back from the slaughtering" (Απού το μακελειό 'ρχεσαι και θα 'σαι κουρασμένος).

Charos' children, Charopoula, appear incidentally, not to say extremely rarely. We find an interesting example in a song from the village Papadatos, close to Xiromero situated in West Greece in the region of Aetolia-Acarnania. The song appears in Motsios' collection (Motsios 216) as well as in the same version in Saunier (Saunier 7δ, p. 160). In the first lines, we come across an intriguing image of the dead singing. Charos reacts with laughter, Charissa with weeping and Charopoula want to lapidate them (Τ' ακούει ο Χάρος και γελάει, η Χάρισσα και κλαίει,/ τ' ακούν και τα Χαρόπουλα και τους λιθοβολάνε).

Among the songs categorized by Saunier into the motif of ransom and redemption (εξαγορά),[392] there is one where the name of Charos' child appears, Charopoulo (Χαρόπουλο). Very precious gifts are being

---

389 See especially the chapter "Hunter, Horseman, Black Rider".

390 In EDT there is an interesting song from Cyprus. It is a dialogue between a young man and Charissa who proposes him to take the gun (πάρε το τουφέκι). His answer reveals the impossibility of such an undertaking, because he now remains in possession of Charos and he has on his breast "black snakes' heads" (μαυρώ φιδκιώ τσεφάλια, EDT 140). The macabre image corresponds exactly with my assumption that it might have been influenced by West European tradition. There are also many other songs containing the snake motif in the eschatological context (EDT 164; 169/ Pasayanis 37; 47; 109; 110).

391 Saunier 1999: 407.

392 Saunier 1999: 189–221.

offered for the three members of Charos' family (a silk dress, a piece of velvet, a golden kerchief) but Charos is incorruptible.[393] A dead man cherishes hope that, thanks to them, he will be given three great Christian feasts in the year (Christmas, Palm Sunday and Easter). All the versions are similar, only the gifts are interchangeable elements:

> Τάξε του Χάρου καμουχά της Χάρισσας βελούδο
> τάξε και του Χαρόπουλου ένα χρυσό μαντήλι. (Saunier 3α, p. 198)
> *Promise Charos silk dresses, Charondissa velvet*
> *promise Charopoulo a golden kerchief.*

> Τάξε του Χάρου καμπουχά, της Χάρισσας βελούδο,
> και του μικρού Χαρόπουλου μεταξωτό μαντήλι. (Pasayanis 45)
> *Promise Charos silk dresses, Charondissa velvet,*
> *promise small Charopoulo a silk kerchief.*

> Τάξε του Χάρου φορεσιά, της Χάρισσας φουστάνι,
> τάξε και του Χαρόπουλου μεταξωτό ζουνάρι. (Spandonidi 218)
> *Promise Charos a uniform, Charondissa a skirt,*
> *and promise Charopoulo a silk belt.*

We come across another similar version, differing in the proposed gifts and this time with the company of Charos' children, in Ioannou:

> Τάξε του Χάρου χάρισμα, της Χάρισσας μαντήλι,
> τάξε και στα Χαρόπουλα όλο φλουριά κι ασήμι. (Ioannou 284)
> *Promise Charos a gift, Charissa a kerchief,*
> *promise Charopoula a lot of gold coins and silver.*

As we have already seen, Charondissa as Charos' mother has absolutely nothing in common with his wife bearing the same name. As a mother, she is personalized and plays a significant role interacting with men – the living as well as the dead. All the characteristics she possesses indicate, in my opinion, that it would not be groundless to regard her as a female counterpart of the male Charos.

Thus her behaviour (warning the living, mercifulness) is highly contrasted with Charos' destroying activity and his cruelties. The question that arises is what could be the reason for the appearance in folk imagination of such a figure in the company of the male personification of death?

---

[393] Dawkins 1942: 139. See also the chapter "Charos' specific characteristics," part "Merchant, Peddler."

I would dare to put forward two hypotheses that at first sight may seem ridiculous, but I am quite convinced are probable, yet difficult to prove. The first one is that Charondissa/Charissa appeared in Greek folk songs due to the grammatical gender of Charos.

The personification of Death and consequently also folk representations are determined by the grammatical gender of the noun "death." In the case of the Greek language, both words defining death, *thanatos* (θάνατος) and Charos (Χάρος) are masculine as in German languages. However, in the Romance as well as in the Slavonic languages, death is always feminine. The phenomenon of grammatical gender and its influence on the representations of death is clearly visible in European art, where death was presented in different masks throughout the centuries. The subject was thoroughly researched, among others, by Białostocki in his essay in which he analyses the metamorphoses of death in European art.[394]

It is noteworthy that, though in German art, death – starting with Holbein – was depicted as an aggressive, lively, strong man, in armour or on horseback,[395] during the nineteenth and twentieth centuries we come across, under Romance and Slavonic languages, female representations of death as a beautiful, seductive woman.[396] Women in the works of the artists from those countries had delicate, captivating female countenance and were full of grace – in contrast to the masculine representations of German origin.[397]

It is very probable that the Modern Greek Charissa/Charondissa was created in the folk imagination just as a female counterpart of the more cruel Charos. It is not as groundless as it seems if we take into account the Slavonic as well as Romance influence on the Hellenic ground over the course of many centuries.

The second hypothesis, which may be seemingly odd, on the presence of a woman in the Underworld is connected with apocryphal

---

[394] I use the Polish edition (Białostocki 2007) of his essay that was originally printed in German, in *Mnemosyne: Festschrift für Manfred Lurker zum 60. Geburtstag*, Baden-Baden, 1988.

[395] Białostocki 2007: 22.

[396] Białostocki 2007: 40.

[397] Białostocki 2007: 28.

Apocalypses, extremely popular in Byzantium, containing the *katabasis* motif.[398] In the texts belonging to this genre, known as *The Apocalypse of the Theotokos*[399] Archangel Michael becomes a guide of the Mother of God.[400] These medieval apocrypha were extremely popular, which may be confirmed by the fact that there are hundreds of manuscripts with the story in ten different languages.[401] All the versions have similar content and are based on the same narrative structures. Characteristically, the Theotokos is presented as a dynamic, active person, who is curious to know all the sins that the sinners suffer from in the other world and is deeply moved by the cruelties the dead experience and is full of compassion for them[402] – similarly to Charondissa in Greek demotic songs. Although it is extremely difficult to prove the interaction of the Mother of God from the apocrypha (also belonging to folk tradition)[403] and the songs in which Charos' mother appears, the assumption I have made is not devoid of any basis.

The context in which Charondissa appears as Charos' potential wife, in comparison with the representations of his mother, seems to belong completely to a different tradition. It has many common features with grotesque and macabre representations known in West European tradition, popular mainly in Baroque art and inspired by medieval rep-

---

[398] The most important surveys of the subject are still: Lambakis 1982, Baun 2007 and Cupane 2014. See also my recent paper Bzinkowski 2015b. It is worth underlining that in Byzantine and post-Byzantine *katabaseis* the descent to the Underworld is reserved almost exclusively to the Mother of God. The other ones may get there only through sleep. Bzinkowski 2015b: 134–137.

[399] Baun analyses thoroughly the manuscripts of *The Apocalypse of Theotokos* from the eleventh until the sixteenth century, especially eight medieval Greek versions. Baun 2007: 40 ff. She pays attention to the fact that some copies of the apocalypse were written by hand in Greece in the nineteenth century and they contain a lot of medieval features. Baun 2007: 40.

[400] In other popular *katabaseis* dating to the tenth century, it is Saint Anastasia guided by Archangel. See Baun 2007: 205.

[401] Baun 2007: 39.

[402] Baun 2007: 274 ff.

[403] It is alluring – yet again not based on any verified proof – to juxtapose the images of Charos' mother crying for the dead, full of compassion Theotokos from the apocryphal apocalypses with the iconographic representations of Virgin Mary known and popular in the Orthodox world as *Lamenting Virgin* (Theotokos Threnousa) and *Virgin of Compassion* (Theotokos Eleousa).

resentations, the interactions of which we come across, as I have mentioned several times, in the works of the Cretan Renaissance.

6. Charos' wedding

The mutual relationship between death and marriage, based both on similarity and opposition, is characteristic to all Indo-European mythologies and is well rooted in European culture.[404] In Ancient Greek literature, especially in tragedy, we find many references to the relation of weddings and funeral, the two ceremonies that conflate and blend together on different levels.[405] The metaphor of death and marriage becomes indeed an attempt to reconcile existing opposition of life and death and, consequently, to come to terms with death, creating a symbolic impression that it is not the end of existence.[406]

As it is attested, there are many parallels in the rituals of weddings and funerals because in popular beliefs they both mark the transition from one stage to another: the dead departs on the last journey and the bride leaves home to start a new life.[407] They both are rites of passage sharing a lot of common features for traditional rural societies in which a wedding turns out to be for close relatives a rather sad occasion since a bride leaves her home for ever to live with her husband.[408]

As Alexiou proved, the Modern Greek laments for the dead are very close structurally and formally to the songs that are sung while a bride leaves her house, similarly as the two rituals that have many parallels.[409] Moreover, as Danforth notes, it is sometimes extremely difficult to clas-

---

404 Giannakis 1998: 93 ff., who analyses the parallelism of "marriage-death" especially on the level of language and according to lexical-cultural semantics.

405 The most comprehensive study on the abundance of the wedding-to-death motif that we find in *Agamemnon* of Aeschylus, but also in Sophocles (*Antigone, Trachniae*) and Eurypides (*Alkestis, Medea, Supplices, Helen, Troades*) was written by Rehm 2004. As for the other Ancient Greek references, see also Giannakis 1998: 94 ff.

406 Danforth 1982: 83.

407 Alexiou 2002b: 120.

408 Danforth 1982: 75.

409 Alexiou 2002b: 120 ff. See also Psychogiou 2008: 48–49.

sify songs as *mirologia* or *nifiatika* (wedding songs), because they strictly depend on the context in which they are performed.[410]

Thus, in demotic songs the phenomenon of death is sometimes conceived as a marriage: if the dead person is a young man it is symbolically expressed by the phrase that "he marries The Black Earth"[411] or just a "gravestone" (πλάκα). The example we find in a song from Pasayanis' collection about dead Andonis who took the gravestone as his mother-in-law and black pebbles for his brothers and cousins:

Ο Αντώνης επαντρεύτηκε κι επήρε μια γυναίκα,
κάνει την πλάκα πεθερά, τη Μαυρηγή γυναίκα,
κι όλα τα μαυροχάλικα αδέρφια και ξαδέρφια. (Pasayanis 116)
Andonis married and took a wife,
he makes the gravestone his mother-in-law, he marries the Black Earth,
and all black pebbles he makes his brothers and cousins.

However, if it is a girl who died, metaphorically her passage to the other world is described as a wedding with Charos. In a song from Cyprus, but widespread throughout Greece and in the Pontus region,[412]

---

[410] Danforth 1982: 74. In the subsequent pages, she deals with songs that are sung both at funerals as well as weddings, showing a lot of analogies between the two rites.

[411] Bzinkowski 2011b: 112. In one of the *mirologia* from Pasayanis there is a short song, where we find the following idea: "Let the Black Earth rejoice [...] who has young men for dancing, young girls for playing" (Η Μαυρηγή να χαίρεται [...] πώχει τους νιους για το χορό, τις νιες για τα παιχνίδια, Pasayanis 91). We also find an interesting example in the collection of songs from Kerkyra, where Charos cooperates with the Black Earth: "Charos and the Black Earth were deliberating on taking my life" (Ο Χάρος με τη μαύρη γης εκάμανε κονσούρτο/ για να μου πάρουν τη ζωή, Paktitis 19), Psychogiou pays attention to the fertility aspect of the Black Earth: "the one who dies symbolically unites with earth that 'devours' him, which can also be understood on a symbolical level as erotic union." Psychogiou 2008: 48. Μαυρηγή becomes in some cases a synonym to Charos as a personification of death: "They call me the Black Earth and blackened gravestone/ I make mothers without sons, women without husbands/ I make black sisters without their brothers." ('Μένα με λένε Μαυρηγής και μαυρισμένη πλάκα/ κάνω μανούλες δίχως γιους, γυναίκες δίχως άντρες/ κάνω και τις μαυραδερφές δίχως τους αδερφούς τους). Cited by Psychogiou 2008: 108. Elsewhere she appears together with Charos: η Μαυρηγής τους τρώει... τα κατσαρά μου τα μαλλιά ο Χάρος τα 'χει πάρει. Cited by Psychogiou 2008: 107. The Black Earth becomes in some cases a synonym to Hades: "What do I need for 'Have a good day' here in the Underworld?/ The place they call here The Black Earth and cobwebbed earth!" (Τι "καλημέρα" θέλω εγώ εδώ στον Κάτου Κόσμο;/ Που εδώ το λένε Μαυρηγής κι αραχλιασμένο χώμα!, Matsinopoulos E-14, β').

[412] Stathis 2004: 818.

Charos appears as a black bird to punish Eugenoulla for her boastfulness. She realizes that she is about to die soon and orders her mother to dress her as a bride because, as she confesses: "I am marrying, I take Charos as a husband" (ωσάν τσ' εώ παντρεύομαι, παίρνω τον Χάρον άντρα, EDT 145; Saunier 19β, p. 410).[413] Thus, in symbolical language, Charos becomes a bridegroom, in other words: taking a young girl by death is conceived as her marriage with Charos.

There are some examples where the wedding ritual is described in more detailed metaphors, like in this fragment from Motsios' collection, where a young girl, who realizes she is about to die soon, asks her mother:

Φέρε μου, μάνα, φέρε μου, το κόκκινο τσεμπέρι,
και προξενιά μου στείλανε ετούτο το σεφέρι,
και προξενιά μου στείλανε να παντρευτώ το Χάρο,
κουμπάρος μας θα' ρθει να μπει ο σκοτεινός ο τάφος. (Motsios 296)
Bring me, my mother, bring me, a red headscarf,
the matchmaking for me it was this journey,
the matchmaking for me it was to marry Charos,
a sombre grave will become for us the best man.

A similar example is found in Sklavenitis' collection, where a girl asks not to tell the guests who will come to her house that she is dying (ψυχομαχεί), but instead they could give her engagement ring to another girl, because she had already become engaged to Charos (εγώ αρρεβωνιάστηκα, πήρα το Χάρο γι' άντρα, Sklavenitis 66).

Sometimes it is the mother who speaks to her daughter, lamenting over her fate and her newly-married husband whom she left for Charos, like in the following "lament song for a bride" (μοιρολόγι σε νύφη) from Northern Epirus:

νέκρωσες τον άντρα σου, Νίκη μου,
που σ' ήθελε πολύ, λουλουδιά μου,
πώς τον άφηκες, Νίκη μου,
και παντρεύτηκες με το Χάρο, λεβέντισσα. (Kapsalis 657)
You put to death your husband, my Niki,
who wanted you so much, my flower,
how did you abandon him, my Niki,
and you married with Charos, you brave young girl.

[413] Bzinkowski 2012: 345.

The motif of the relationship between death and marriage may also be illustrated by different kinds of imagery. The folk imagination transferred the idea of wedding to Charos' family. In this case, it is not Charos who is the bridegroom, but Charos who marries his son (παντρεύει τον υγιό του). On that occasion, he invites all the dead to take part in the Underworld ceremony[414]:

κάνει ο Χάρος μια χαρά,[415] παντρεύει τον υγιό του.
Καλεί τους νιους για το χορό, τις νιες για το τραγούδι,
καλεί και τα μικρά παιδιά για τις απόκρισές του. (Kondomichis 6, p. 172)
Charos makes a feast, he marries his son.
He calls young boys for dancing, young girls for singing,
he calls little children so that they serve him.

In Matsinopoulos' versions, the first two verses are almost the same, yet the last one differs:

καλεί και τα μικρά παιδιά, λουλούδια να του πάνε. (Matsinopoulos Δ-7, α')
κι αυτούς τους πρωτογέροντες για τα χρυσά τραπέζια
κι τα μικρούλια τα παιδιά, να νεκροκουβαλάνε (Matsinopoulos Δ-7, β')
He also invites little children, so that they bring him flowers,
and these first old men to golden tables.
He also calls little children to serve the dead.

In another version, Charos "calls for assembly" in order to marry his son:

Ο Χάρος κάνει σύναξη του γιου του για το γάμο,
διαλέει νιους για το χορό και νιες για το τραπέζι. (Kondomichis 17, p. 175)
Charos calls for assembly on the occasion of his son's wedding,
he chooses young boys for dances, young girls for the table.

Or "calls all the people":

Εκάλεσε ούλο το ντουνιά, ούλη την οικουμένη. (Matsinopoulos Δ-7, ε')
He invited all the people, all the world.

---

414 Close to that representation is also the motif of dining with Charos. The dead – usually young girls and boys – are then invited to eat with him. See Matsinopoulos Δ-8, α', β'). See also Borowska 2008: 85–86.

415 This is one of the most common word plays, rather untranslatable, based on the similarity of the words Χάρος (*Charos*) and χαρά (*chara* – joy). There are countless folk songs in which the phrase appears, among others, we come across it [in:] Motsios 253, p. 241; Saunier 7β, p. 302; 7στ, p. 304; 7η, p. 306; 7ια, p. 308; Saunier 7ε, p. 304; Saunier 7θ, p. 306; Saunier 7δ, p. 304. Similarly, Charos is sometimes called άχαρος (*acharos*) – unpleasing, graceless. (Saunier 4, p. 200).

In the context of Charos' son's wedding, the well-known garden imagery connected rather with the motif of Charos the builder also appears:

Καλεί τις νιες για λεϊμονιές, τους νιους για κυπαρίσσια,
καλεί και τα μικρά παιδιά, όλο χαμομηλίτσες. (Matsinopoulos Δ-7, γ')
He invites young girls as lemon trees, young boys as cypresses,
he invites little children, as small apple trees.

The death of someone is sometimes explained by the necessity of gathering the guests for Charos' son's wedding. Interestingly, he does not need only young girls and boys as usual, but also the old "to slaughter them like rams":

Ο Χάρος τον εκάλεσε, παντρεύει τον υγιό του.
Καλεί τους νιους για το χορό, τις νιες για τα τραγούδια,
μαζεύει και τους γέροντες, να σφάξη για κριάρια. (Pasayanis 93)
Charos invited him, he marries his son.
He invites young boys for dances, young girls for songs,
he also gathers the old to slaughter them as rams.

The close interrelationship between death and marriage and, consequently, between funeral laments and wedding songs with many resemblances, is not exclusively a Hellenic concept and is widespread in the whole Balkan region.[416] However, it is worth underlining that the above-mentioned examples show some characteristics that are uniquely of Greek origin and do not appear in the folk songs of other countries. These are the concepts of Charos as a bridegroom and the idea of wedding in the lower world.

The linguistic representation of this concept is expressed by the phrases used in reference to young girls, such as: "I take Charos as a husband" (παίρνω το Χάρο άντρα) or "I marry Charos" (παντρεύομαι [με] το Χάρο). The wedding in Hades seems to be an elaboration of the same

[416] Alexiou 2002b: 120–122; 230 (footnote 64). Such parallels are present, among others, in the folk songs of Hungary, Bulgaria and Romania. They concern mostly the funerals of unmarried people. Danforth refers to an interesting custom when the remains of an unmarried person are exhumed. The ceremony looks like it was a greeting of a bride and groom. The laments that are sung at the exhumation describe the departure of the bride from her home. Significantly in the lament songs cited by Danforth Charos is the one who tries to hold back the person whose remains are exhumed. Danforth 1982: 85–89.

idea, enriched by an eschatological aspect characteristic to Greek folk beliefs, namely the abode of all the dead. The picture that appears in this case seems to be a mirror image of the hypothetical wedding that could take place in the upper world. The parallels on a linguistic as well as symbolic and ritual level indicate that the parallel "marriage–death" (γάμος–θάνατος) is not just a poetic concept and invention of those performing *mirologia*, but is deeply rooted in folk thinking and goes back to the most archaic and universal ideas known from antiquity. The figure of Charos in this context becomes not just a simple personification of death, nor the Angel of death executing God's orders or his own duties,[417] but constitutes rather a symbolic representation of ancient dualistic thinking, according to which death and marriage are two sides of the same aspect – departing and passage, understood symbolically and metaphorically.

---

[417] I disagree with Psychogiou (2008: 27) in this point and I think Charos in the wedding motif is as important as the Black Earth in reference to the vegetation symbolism. Moreover, it is Charos that is used in association with reaping and harvesting in demotic songs rather than his female counterpart in the figure of the Black Earth as mother-earth, who is present rather in rituals than in the texts.

CONCLUSION

Since the figure of Charos, as we have seen, is not a homogeneous mythological personage in demotic songs and is characterized by a wide variety of representations, in many cases not coherent with each other, it is all but impossible to attempt to embrace the whole range of them in a unified way. Although the name of Charos appears almost exclusively in the eschatological context and in some unquestionable cases may be identified as a folk personification of Death or God's messenger, the Angel of Death, all the above-mentioned examples prove that any unequivocal characterisation of his appearance as well as of his activities is doomed to failure.

Moreover, as I have already stressed, the similarity of his name to the ancient ferryman of the dead brought about many misinterpretations and misunderstandings regarding some aspects of Charos' images. Yet, as it turns out after closer examination and comparison of different variants of the same motives, it is very hard to find an obvious confirmation anywhere in demotic songs that Charos leads the dead to the Underworld. Undoubtedly, as is visible through the analysis of some common phrases of demotic songs as well as of the representations of him as an aggressor and the lord in the world below, according to the folk view, he indeed is responsible for "taking" lives, usually of those prematurely dead, children and young people. However, the other representations that I have outlined, such as of Charos the builder and the gardener or Charos as a bridegroom, clearly show that in this figure from folk mythology a whole cosmos of multi-layered concepts is hidden, some of them going back to the most archaic symbolic thinking.

The attempt to analyse the complex personality of Charos in demotic songs also distinctly reveals countless possible intercultural interferences that contributed to the creation of such intangible and enigmatic representations. Since, as I have demonstrated, many of Charos' images bring to mind some concepts unknown in Byzantium or Modern Greece, but present in the cultural traditions of West Europe, in order to trace their possible sources it seemed relevant to allude to cultures that had been in constant contact in the course of centuries with the Hellenic lands. The external influences, as I attempted to show, concern not exclusively the reception of some ideas in literature, as is clearly visible in the case of the works written during the Cretan Renaissance, but, most importantly, the transmission of ideas that mingled with Greek concepts, creating a unique composition, a mosaic, the shape and colours of which are never fully static and discernible.

The case of Charos and his different manifestations clearly proves that Greek folk culture cannot be fully separated from written and learned tradition, which is a characteristic feature of all European countries.[418] Both traditions always permeated each other, borrowing not only from themselves but also from every cultural manifestation and idea they had contact with. Thus, as our example of Charos in Greek demotic songs, which are treated significantly as written literature, confirms, the most characteristic feature for the texts belonging to folk songs is exactly what we could call a variety. Popular culture was never homogeneous and uniform and was always susceptible to the influences of "high" culture and learned literature.[419] Any approach to the mythological motives that demotic songs convey, usually through the language of hidden and veiled imagery, should then include references to the literary works of different epochs and, in some cases, of external traditions whose ideas have been transmitted for centuries. Some traces of ancient concepts and the works of Byzantine and post-Byzantine periods, as well as of the Cretan Renaissance, that I linked with the figure of Charos in demotic songs prove the above-mentioned suggestion about the interference of ideas. Unfortunately, they also attest our impossibility of tracing them exactly and without any doubt due to the lack of obvious evidence.

However, the eschatological context in which the enigmatic figure of Charos mostly manifests himself is very specific and fragile, as it reflects one of the most universal spheres of experience common to all human

418 Puchner 2009: 142.

419 Burke 1978: 21–22.

beings. Modern Greek demotic songs may constitute confirmation that the old, most archaic ideas concerning the afterlife beliefs are insignificantly vulnerable to later cultural influences. The most ancient concepts not only coexist with the eschatology of Orthodox Christianity but, as the case of Modern Greek folk songs convincingly demonstrates, are even more vital and meaningful for the Greeks than the Christian ones.

Charos from demotic songs, as it results from the characteristics outlined above, turns out to be not a single mythological personage embodying one particular idea manifesting himself in different ways and through different imagery. Based on the variety of his representations, one cannot shake the impression that through the various masks that are put onto his name echoing the ancient ferryman of the dead, we could discern miscellaneous concepts and ideas related to the eschatology of the individual according to the folk world view.

BIBLIOGRAPHY

Collections of folk songs:

(Abbot) Abbot G.F., 1900, *Songs of modern Greece*, Cambridge.

(Chasiotis) Chasiotis G. Χασιώτης Γ., 1866, *Συλλογή των κατά την Ήπειρον δημοτικών ασμάτων*, Εν Αθήναις.

(Daraki) Daraki P. Δαράκη Π., 1972, *Τραγούδια της Αγίας Παρασκευής της Λέσβου*, Αθήνα.

(Detorakis) Detorakis Th. Δετοράκης Θ., 1976, *Ανέκδοτα δημοτικά τραγούδια της Κρήτης*, Ηράκλειο.

(EDT) *Ελληνικά Δημοτικά Τραγούδια*, 1947, τ. Α', Ακαδημία Αθηνών.

(Fauriel) Fauriel C.Ch., 1824–1825, *Chants populaires de la Grèce moderne*, Paris.

(Garnett) Garnett L.M.J., 1888, *Greek folk-songs from the Ottoman provinces of Northern Hellas*, London.

(Gneutos) Gneutos P. Γνευτός Π., 1980, *Τραγούδια δημοτικά της Ρόδου*, Ρόδος.

(Hahn) Hahn J.G. von, 1864, *Griechische und albanesische Märchen*, Leipzig.

(Iatridis) Iatridis A. Ιατρίδης Α., 1859, *Συλλογή δημοτικών ασμάτων. Παλαιών και νέων. Μετά διαφόρων Εικονογραφιών*, Εν Αθήναις.

(Ioannou) Ioannou G. Ιωάννου Γ., 1994, *Τα δημοτικά μας τραγούδια*, Αθήνα.

(Kanellakis) Kanellakis K. Κανελλάκης Κ., 1890, *Χιακά Ανάλεκτα, ήτοι σύλλογοι ηθών, εθίμων, παροιμιών, δημωδών ασμάτων, αινιγμάτων, λεξιλογίου, ιστορικών και άλλων χειρογράφων, χρυσοβούλλων, σιγιλλίων κλπ.*, Εν Αθήναις.

(Kapsalis) Kapsalis G.D. Καψάλης Γ.Δ, 2003, *Δημοτικά τραγούδια από τη Βόρειο Ήπειρο*, Αθήνα.

(Katsalidas) Katsalidas G.N. Κατσαλίδας Γ.Ν., 2001, *Δημοτικά τραγούδια από τη Βόρειο Ήπειρο*, Αθήνα.

(Kind) Kind T., 1861, *Anthologie neugriechischer Volkslieder*, Leipzig.

(Kitromilidou) Kitromilidou M.M. Κιτρομηλίδου Μ.Μ., 1990, *Ακριτικά τραγούδια και παραλογές από την Κύπρο*, Λευκωσία.

(Kondomichis) Kondomichis P. Κοντομίχης Π., 1985, *Δημοτικά τραγούδια της Λευκάδας*, Αθήνα.

(Koridis) Koridis G. Κορίδης Γ., 2002, *Τα ωραιότερα δημοτικά τραγούδια. Δ' Τόμος. Μοιρολόγια-Της Ξενιτιάς-Παραλογές*, Αθήνα.

(Kougeas) Kougeas S. Κουγέας Σ., 2000, *Τραγούδια του κάτω κόσμου. Μοιρολόγια της Μεσσηνιακής Μάνης, συλλογή του ακαδημαϊκού Σωκράτη Κουγέα, κατά τα έτη 1901–1904*, Αθήνα.

(Kriaris) Kriaris A. Κριάρης Α., 1920, *Πλήρης Συλλογή Κρητικών ασμάτων: ηρωικών, ιστορικών, πολεμικών, του γάμου, της τάβλας, του χορού κλπ. και απασών των κρητικών παροιμιών διστίχων και αινιγμάτων μεθ' ερμηνευτικών υποσημειώσεων*, Εν Αθήναις.

(Lagarde) Lagarde P. de, 1886, *NeuGriechisches aus Klein Asien*, Göttingen.

(Legrand) Legrand É., 1874, *Recueil de chansons populaires grecques*, Paris.

(Lévy) Lévy M., 1860, *Chants populaires de la Grèce moderne*, Paris.

(Makris) Makris M. Μακρής Μ., 1983, *Δωδεκανησιακά δημοτικά τραγούδια*, Ρόδος.

(Manolakakis) Manolakakis E. Μανωλακάκης Ε., 1896, *Καρπαθιακά*, Αθήνα.

(Marcellus) Marcellus M. de, 1851, *Chants du peuple on Grèce*, 2 vol., Paris.

(Markos) Markos K. Μάρκος Κ., 1999, *Ακριτικά δημοτικά τραγούδια. Σε βυζαντινή και Ευρωπαϊκή μουσική σημειογραφία*. Πρώτος τόμος, Αθήνα.

(Matsinopoulos) Matsinopoulos V.P. Ματσινόπουλος Β.Π., 2008, *Μοιρολόγια Τριφυλίας – Νοτιοδυτικής Πελοποννήσου με παραλλαγές λοιπής Ελλάδος και παραπομπές στον Όμηρο*, Αθήνα.

(Michailidis-Nouaros) Michailidis-Nouaros A. Μιχαηλίδης-Νουάρος Α., 2007, *Δημοτικά τραγούδια Καρπάθου*, Αθήνα.

(Motsios) Motsios G. Μότσιος Γ., 1995, *Το ελληνικό μοιρολόγι*, Αθήνα.

(Müller) Müller W., 1825, *Neugriechische Volkslieder*, Leipzig.

(Nimas) Nimas Th.A. Νήμας Θ.Α., 1981, *Δημοτικά τραγούδια της Θεσσαλίας*, Θεσσαλονίκη.

(Paktitis) Paktitis N.A. Πακτίτης Ν.Α, 1989, *Κερκυραϊκά Δημοτικά τραγούδια*, Αθήνα.

(Pasayanis) Pasayanis K., Πασαγιάννης Κ., 1928, *Μανιάτικα μοιρολόγια και τραγούδια*, Αθήνα.

(Passow) Passow A., 1860, *Popularia carmina graeciae recentioris*, Lipsiae.

(Petropoulos) Petropoulos D. Πετρόπουλος Δ., 1958–1959, Ελληνικά Δημοτικά Τραγούδια, τομ. Β', Αθήνα.

(Politis, a) Politis N., 1914, Πολίτης Ν., *Εκλογαί από τα τραγούδια του ελληνικού λαού*, Εν Αθήναις.

(Politis, b) Politis N., 1909, Πολίτης Ν., *Ακριτικά άσματα: Ο θάνατος του Διγενή*, Εν Αθήναις.

(Sakellarios, a) Sakellarios A. Σακελλάριος Α., 1868, *Τα Κυπριακά. Τόμος τρίτος*, Εν Αθήναις.

(Sakellarios, b) Sakellarios A. Σακελλάριος Α., 1891, *Τα Κυπριακά: Ήτοι Γεωγραφία, Ιστορία και Γλώσσα της Κύπρου από των αρχαιοτάτων χρόνων μέχρι σήμερον*, τ. 2, Εν Αθήναις.

(Saunier) Saunier G., 1999, *Ελληνικά δημοτικά τραγούδια. Τα μοιρολόγια*, Αθήνα.

(Schmidt) Schmidt B., 1877, *Griechische Märchen, Sagen und Volkslieder*, Leipzig.

(Sheridan) Sheridan C.B., 1825, *The Songs of Greece, translated from the Romaic text edited by M.C. Fauriel, with additions*, London.
(Sklavenitis) Sklavenitis D.Ch. Σκλαβενίτης Δ.Χ., 2012, *Μοιρολόγια Πόρου Λευκάδας*. Καταγραφή, μελέτη, υπομνηματισμός: Χριστόφορος Δ. Σκλαβενίτης, Αφηγήτρια: Ιωάννα Β. Μεταξά, Πρόλογος: Guy (Michel) Saunier, Επιμέλεια: Τριαντάφυλλος Ε. Σκλαβενίτης, Αθήνα.
(Spandonidi) Spandonidi E. Σπανδωνίδη Ε., 1939, *Τα Τραγούδια της Αγόριανης*, Αθήνα.
(Theros) Theros A. Θέρος Α., 1952, *Τα τραγούδια των Ελλήνων*, τ. Β', Αθήνα.
(Tomasseo) Tommaseo N., 1842, *Canti popolari italiani, corsi, illirici, greci*, vol. III, Venezia.
(Tsouderos) Tsouderos G.E. Τσουδερός Γ.Ε., 1986, *Μεσσηνιακά μοιρολόγια: Κυπαρισσία και περίχωρα*, Αθήνα.
(Vanglis) Vanglis S.A. Βαγγλής Σ.Α., 1986, *Τα δημοτικά τραγούδια της Χαλκιδικής*, Θεσσαλονίκη.
(Zambelios) Zambelios S. Ζαμπέλιος Σ., 1852, *Άσματα δημοτικά της Ελλάδος: Εκδοθέντα μετά μελέτης ιστορικής περί μεσαιωνικού Ελληνισμού*, Κέρκυρα.

Dictionaries:

(Babiniotis) Babiniotis G. Μπαμπινιώτης Γ., 2002, *Λεξικό της νέας ελληνικής γλώσσας*, Αθήνα.
(Charalambakis) Charalambakis Ch.G. Χαραλαμπάκης Χ.Γ., 2014, *Χρηστικό λεξικό της νεοελληνικής γλώσσας*, Αθήνα.
(Dimitrakos) Dimitrakos D.V. Δημητράκος Δ.Β., 1958, *Μέγα λεξικόν όλης της ελληνικής γλώσσης*, Αθήναι.
(Mandala) Mandala M. Μανδαλά Μ., 2002, *Μείζον ελληνικό λεξικό* (Τρίτη έκδοση), Αθήνα.
(Stamatakos) Stamatakos I. Σταματάκος Ι., 1952–1955, *Λεξικόν της Νέας Ελληνικής Γλώσσης*, Αθήναι.
(Stavropoulos) Stavropoulos D.N., 1996, *Oxford Greek-English Learner's Dictionary*, Oxford.

Secondary literature:

Abbot G.F., 1903, *Macedonian folklore*, Cambridge.
Alexiou M., 1978, "Modern Greek Folklore and Its Relations to the Past: The Evolution of Charos in Greek Tradition", [in:] S. Vryonis (ed.), *The "Past" in Medieval and Modern Greek Culture*, Malibu, California, 211–236.
Alexiou M., 1984–1985, "Folklore, an Obituary," *BMGS* 9, 1–29.

Alexiou M., 2002a, *After Antiquity: Greek Language, Myth, and Metaphor*, Ithaca.
Alexiou M., 2002b, *Ritual Lament in Greek Tradition*, rev. D. Yatromanolakis, P. Roilos, Cambridge.
Alexiou St., Aposkiti M. Αλεξίου Στ., Αποσκίτη Μ., 1988, *Ἐρωφίλη τραγωδία Γεωργίου Χορτάτση*, Αθήνα.
Anagnostopoulos I.Sp. Αναγνωστόπουλος Ι.Σπ., 1984, *Ο θάνατος και ο κάτω κόσμος στη δημοτική ποίηση. Εσχατολογία της δημοτικής ποίησης*, Αθήνα.
Angold M., 2000, *Church and Society in Byzantium under the Comneni, 1081 -1261*, Cambridge.
Ariès P., 2011, *Człowiek i śmierć*, Warszawa. [Originally published as: *L' homme devant la mort*, Paris 1977 et 1985.]
Avdikos E., 2010, "Continuity, Identity and Folk Studies in Greece," *Folklore. Electronic Journal of Folklore* 44, 157–170.
Bakker Wim F., Gemert Arnold F. van, 2008, *Ρίμα θρηνητική εις τον πικρόν και ακόρεστον Άδην. Ποίημα κυρ-Ιωάννου Πικατόρου εκ πόλεως Ρηθύμνης*: Κριτική έκδοση, Πανεπιστημιακές Εκδόσεις Κρήτης.
Bartmiński J., 1996, *Słownik stereotypów i symboli ludowych T. I, 1*, Lublin.
Bartmiński J., 1999, *Słownik stereotypów i symboli ludowych T. I, 2*, Lublin.
Baun J., 2007, *Tales from Another Byzantium: Celestial journey and local community in the medieval Greek apocrypha*, Cambridge.
Beaton R., 1981, "'Digenes Akrites' and Modern Greek Folksongs: A Reassessement," *Byzantion* 51, 22–43.
Beaton R., 1986, *The Oral Traditions of Modern Greece: A Survey*, Oral Tradition 1/1, 110–133.
Beaton R., 2004, *Folk Poetry of Modern Greece*, Cambridge.
Bernstein A.E., 2006, *Jak powstało piekło. Śmierć i zadośćuczynienie w świecie starożytnym oraz początkach chrześcijaństwa*, Kraków. [Originally published as: *The Formation of Hell: Death and Retribution in the Ancient and Early Christian Worlds*, New York 1993.]
Białostocki J., 2007, *Płeć śmierci*, Gdańsk. [Originally published as: *Mnemosyne: Festschrift für Manfred Lurker zum 60. Geburtstag*, Baden-Baden, 1988.]
Blažek V., 2007, "Theonymica Helleno-Semitica I. Charon," *DO-MO-SO. Fascicula Mycenologica et Classica Polona* 7, 155–159.
Borowska M., 2004, *Arcydzieła literatury nowogreckiej. Tom II. Gminna pieśń Greków. Antologia. Wybrała, przełożyła, wstępem i komentarzem opatrzyła Małgorzata Borowska*, Warszawa.
Borowska M., 2008, "Charos-Śmierć i obraz Zaświatów w nowogreckiej pieśni gminnej," [in:] J. Olko (ed.), *Obrzęd, teatr, ceremoniał w dawnych kulturach*, Warszawa, 77–86.
Borowska M., 2011, „Ogrody Charosa. Ogród i śmierć w wybranych utworach poezji nowogreckiej," *Prace Filologiczne* 1, 119–134.
Burke P., 1978, *Popular Culture in Early Modern Europe*, New York.
Bylina S., 1999, *Kultura ludowa Polski i Słowiańszczyzny średniowiecznej*, Warszawa.

Bzinkowski M., 2009, "Charos Psychopompos? Tracing the Continuity of the Idea of a Ferryman of the Dead in Greek Culture," *Classica Cracoviensia* XIII, 17–33.

Bzinkowski M., 2011a, "Στο περιβόλι του Χάρου – εσχατολογική ταυτότητα στα δημοτικά τραγούδια," [in:] *Πρακτικά του Τέταρτου Συνεδρίου της Ευρωπαϊκής Εταιρείας Νεοελληνικών Σπουδών 'Ταυτότητες στον ελληνικό κόσμο (από το 1204 έως σήμερα),'* Επιμ. Κ. Δημάδης, Τόμος Β΄, Γρανάδα, 441–454.

Bzinkowski M., 2011b, "Names of the Abode of the Dead in Modern Greek Folk Songs," *Živa Antika* 61, 101–115.

Bzinkowski M., 2012, "Bird Imagery in Eschatological Landscape of Modern Greek Funeral Laments," *EOS* 99/2, 2012, 337–358.

Bzinkowski M., 2015a, "The Case of the Angels. The Relevance of the Research by Classical Scholar John Cuthbert Lawson (1874–1919) on Modern Greek Culture," *Classica Cracoviensia* 2015, vol. 18, 83–110.

Bzinkowski M., 2015b, "Notes on Eschatological Patterns in a 12th century Anonymous Satirical Dialogue the 'Timarion,'" *EOS* 102/1, 2015, 129–148.

Bzinkowski M., Serrano M., 2015, "Η δυτικοευρωπαϊκή μάσκα του Χάρου στα δημοτικά τραγούδια," [in:] *Πρακτικά Ε΄ Ευρωπαϊκού Συνεδρίου Νεοελληνικών Σπουδών, Τόμος Ε΄*, Επιμ. Κ. Δημάδης, Αθήνα, 807–828.

Constantelos D., 1996, *Christian Hellenism: Essays and Studies in Continuity and Change*, New Rochelle, NY.

Cupane C., 2014, "The Heavenly City: Religious and Secular Visions of the Other World in Byzantine Literature," [in:] Ch. Angelidi and G.T. Calofonos (eds.), *Dreaming in Byzantium and Beyond*. Oxford, 53–68.

Danforth L., 1982, *The Death Rituals of Rural Greece*, New Jersey.

Dawkins R.M., 1916, *Modern Greek in Asia Minor: A Study of the Dialects of Sílli, Cappadocia and Phárasa, with Grammar, Texts, Translations and Glossary*, Cambridge.

Dawkins R.M., 1942, "Soul and Body in the Folklore of Modern Greece," *Folklore* 53/3, 131–147.

Dawkins R.M., 1953, *Modern Greek folktales*, Oxford.

Dimaras K.Th. Δημαράς Κ.Θ., 1987, *Ιστορία της νεοελληνικής λογοτεχνίας*, Αθήνα.

Dimitrova N., 2002, "Inscriptions and Iconography in the Monuments of the Thracian Rider," *Hesperia* 71, iss. 2, 209–229.

Dyer L., 1891, *Studies of the Gods in Greece at Certain Sanctuaries Recently Excavated*, New York.

Geldart E.M., 1884, *Folk-lore of Modern Greece*, London.

Gemert A. van, 1991, "Literary Antecedents," [in:] D. Holton (ed.), *Literature and Society in Renaissance Crete*, Cambridge, 49–78.

Giannakis G.K. Γιαννάκης Γ.Κ, 1998, *Το ποιητικό μοτίβο 'γάμος – θάνατος' στην αρχαία ελληνική και την ινδοευρωπαϊκή*, ΔΩΔΩΝΗ – 'Φιλολογία' 27, 93–113.

Håland E.J., 2014, *Rituals of Death and Dying in Modern and Ancient Greece: Writing History from a Female Perspective*, Cambridge.

Hamilton G.L., 1912, "Modern Greek Folklore and Ancient Greek Religion: A Study in Survivals by John Cuthbert Lawson" [Rev.], *The American Journal of Philology* 33/1, 87–90.

Harisson J.E., 1910, "Modern Greek Folklore and Ancient Greek Religion: A Study in Survivals. By John Cuthbert Lawson" [Rev.], *The Classical Review* 24/6, 181–183.

Hartnup K., 2004, *On the Beliefs of the Greeks: Leo Allatios and Popular Orthodoxy*, Leiden–Boston.

Herzfeld M., 1982, *Ours Once More: Folklore, Ideology and the Making of Modern Greece*, New York.

Hesseling D.C., 1897, *Charos. Ein Beitrag zur Kentniss des Neugriechischen Volksglaubens*, Leiden–Leipzig.

Hesseling D.C., 1931, "Le Charos byzantine," *Neophilologus* 16: 131–135.

Holst-Warhaft G., 1992, *Dangerous Voices: Women's Laments and Greek Literature*, London.

Homer, *The Odyssey* with an English Translation by A.T. Murray, text accessible on: http://www.perseus.tufts.edu/.

Hutter M., Sikke Y. de, 1979, "Le chant du destin. Quelques aspects de la conception de la mort en Grece à travers les 'miriologues,'" [in:] *Les hommes et la mort. Rituels funéraires a travers le monde*, textes rassemblés et présentés par J. Guiart, Paris, 59–71.

Ibrovac M., 1966, *Claude Fauriel et la fortune européenne des poésies populaires grecque et serbe: étude d'histoire romantique, suivie du Cours de Fauriel la Poésie populaire des Serbes et des Grecs, professé en Sorbonne 1831–1832*, Paris.

Janion M., 1973, *Demony morza*, [intr. to] Frederick Marryat, *Okręt widmo*, Gdańsk, 5–22.

Johnston P.S., 2010, *Cienie Szeolu. Śmierć i zaświaty w biblijnej tradycji żydowskiej*, Kraków. [Originally published as: *Shades of Sheol. Death and Afterlife in the Old Testament*, Nottingham 2002.]

Kakridis J.Th., 1969, "John Cuthbert Lawson: Modern Greek Folklore and Ancient Greek Religion: A study in Survivals. Foreword by A.N. Oikonomides" [Rev.], *Gnomon* 41, 495–499.

Kambouroglou D., 1889, Καμπούρογλου Δ., *Ιστορία των Αθηναίων: Τουρκοκρατία: Περίοδος πρώτη, 1458–1687*, εκδίδοται υπό Α. Παπαγεωργίου, τ. 1, Εν Αθήναις.

Kapsomenos E. Καψωμένος Ε., 1995, *Δημοτικό τραγούδι. Μια διαφορετική προσέγγιση*, Αθήνα.

Knös B., 1962, "L'histoire de la littérature néo-grecque," *Acta Universitatis Upsalensis. Studia Graeca Upsaliensia* 1, Stockholm.

Kosegian Ch., Κοσεγιάν Χ., 2010, *Αρχαία επιβιώματα στα νεοελληνικά δημοτικά τραγούδια*, Αθήνα.

Kougeas S. Κουγέας Σ., 2000, *Τραγούδια του κάτω κόσμου. Μοιρολόγια της Μεσσηνιακής Μάνης, συλλογή του ακαδημαϊκού Σωκράτη Κουγέα, κατά τα έτη 1901–1904*, Αθήνα.
Krueger D., 2006, *Byzantine Christianity*, vol. III, Minneapolis.
Kyriakidis S. Κυριακίδης Σ., 1978, *Το δημοτικό τραγούδι*, Αθήνα.
Kyriakidou-Nestoros A. Κυριακίδου-Νέστορος Α., 1978, *Η θεωρία της ελληνικής λαογραφίας. Κριτική Ανάλυση*, Αθήνα.
Lambakis S., 1982, Λαμπάκης Σ., *Οι καταβάσεις στον Κάτω Κόσμο στη βυζαντινή και στη μεταβυζαντινή λογοτεχνία*, Αθήνα.
Lawson J.C., 1910, *Modern Greek Folklore and Ancient Greek Religion*, Cambridge.
Legrand E., Pernot H., 1899, *Chrestomanie grecque moderne*, Garnier.
Mackridge P., 2009, "From Archaeology to Dialectology and Folklore: The Role of the British School at Athens in the Career of R. M. Dawkins," *British School at Athens Studies* 17, 49–58.
Mavrogordato J., 1955, "Modern Greek Folksongs of the Dead," *Journal of Hellenic Studies* 75, 42–53.
Merchiers I., 2007, *Cultural Nationalism in the South Slav Habsburg Lands in the Early Nineteenth Century: The Scholary Network of Jernej Kopitar (1780 –1844)*, Slavistische Beiträge, Band 455, München.
Meyendorff J., 1979, *Byzantine Theology: Historical Trends and Doctrinal Themes*, New York.
Michailidis-Nouaros M.G., 1932, *Λαογραφικά Σύμμεικτα Καρπάθου*, Αθήνα.
Moore C.H., 1912, "Modern Greek Folklore and Ancient Greek Religion by John Cuthbert Lawson" [Rev.], *Classical Philology* 7/1 , 108–111.
Moore C.H., 1916, *The Religious Thought of the Greeks: From Homer to the Triumph of Christianity*, Cambridge.
Moravcsik G., 1931, "Il Caronte bizantino," *Studi Bizantini e Neoellenici* 3, 47–68.
Omatos O., 1990, "Del Caronte Barquero al Jaros neohelénico," *Veleia* 7, 303–316.
Panagiotakes N.M., 1995, "The Italian Background of Early Cretan Literature," *Dumbarton Oaks Papers*, vol. 49. *Symposium on Byzantium and the Italians, 13th–15th Centuries*, 281–323.
Parédes A., 1965, "Modern Greek Folklore and Ancient Greek Religion: A Study in Survivals. By John Cuthbert Lawson," new foreword by A.N. Oikonomides, *Journal of American Folklore* 78/310, 356.
Peers G., 2001, *Subtle Bodies: Representing Angels in Byzantium (The Transformation of the Classical Heritage)*, Oakland.
Pernot H., 1931, *Chansons populaires grecques des XVe et XVIe siècles publiées et traduites*. Paris.
Politis L., 1973, *A History of Modern Greek Literature*, Oxford.
Politis N. Πολίτης Ν., 1882, *Ο ήλιος κατά τους δημώδεις μύθους*, Εν Αθήναις.
Politis N. Πολίτης Ν., 1909, *Ακριτικά άσματα: Ο θάνατος του Διγενή*, Εν Αθήναις.

Politis N. Πολίτης N., 1874, *Μελέτη επί του βίου των νεωτέρων Ελλήνων*. Τόμος Πρώτος. *Νεοελληνική μυθολογία* [Μέρος Β'], Εν Αθήναις.

Politis A. Πολίτης A., 2011, *Το δημοτικό τραγούδι*, Ηράκλειο.

Prioreschi P., 1990, *A History of Human Responses to Death: Mythologies, Rituals and Ethics (Studies in Health & Human Services)*, Lewinston.

Przymuszała L., 2007, "Narodziny i śmierć we frazeologii gwarowej," [in:] *Frazeologia a językowe obrazy świata przełomu wieków*, [in:] W. Chlebda (ed.), Opole, 105–110.

Psychogiou E., Ψυχογιού E., 2008, *'Μαυρηγή' και Ελένη. Τελετουργίες θανάτου και αναγέννησης*, Εν Αθήναις.

Puchner W., 2009, *Θεωρητική λαογραφία. Έννοιες, μέθοδοι, θεματικές*, Αθήνα.

Rehm R., 1994, *Marriage to Death: The Conflation of Wedding and Funeral Rituals in Greek Tragedy*, New Jersey.

Riasanovsky N.V., 2005, *Russian Identities: A Historical Survey*, Oxford.

Rodd R., 1892, *The Customs and the Lore of Modern Greece*, London.

Roilos P. Ροϊλός Π., 1998, *Ο νεκρός ως δέντρο στα ελληνικά μοιρολόγια*, Ελληνικά τ. 48, τεύχος 1, 61–85.

Romaios K. Ρωμαίος K., 1979, *Δημοτικό τραγούδι Α': Προβλήματα καταγωγής και τεχνοτροπίας*, Αθήνα.

Rose H.J., 1910, "Modern Greek Folklore and Ancient Greek Religion: A Study in Survivals. By John Cuthbert Lawson" [Rev.], *Folk-Lore* XXI, 529–532.

Rose H.J., "Charon: Charos," *Folklore*, vol. 24, no. 2, 1913, 247.

Sacha-Piekło M. (ed.), 1999, *Zaświaty i krainy mityczne*, Kraków.

Saunier G., 1972, "Le combat avec Charos dans les chansons populaires grecques. Formes originelles et formes dérivées," *Ελληνικά* 25, 119–152, 335–370.

Saunier G., 1979, *"Adikia." Le mal et l'injustice dans les chansons populaires grecques*, Paris.

Saunier G., 1982, "Charos et l'Histoire dans les chansons populaires grecques," *Revue des Études Grecques* 95, 297–321.

Saunier G., 1993, "Is There Such a Thing as an 'Acritic Song'"? Problems in Classification of Modern Greek Narrative Songs", [in:] Beaton R., Ricks D., *Digenes Akrites: New Approaches to Byzantine Heroic Poetry*, London, 139–149.

Saunier G., 1999, *Ελληνικά δημοτικά τραγούδια. Τα μοιρολόγια*, Αθήνα.

Schmidt B., 1871, *Das Volksleben der Neugriechen und das hellenische Alterthum*, Leipzig.

Seremetakis C.N., 1991, *The Last Word: Women, Death, and Divination in Inner Mani*, Chicago.

Sklavenitis D.Ch. Σκλαβενίτης Δ. Χ., 2012, *Μοιρολόγια Πόρου Λευκάδας*. Καταγραφή, μελέτη, υπομνηματισμός: Χριστόφορος Δ. Σκλαβενίτης, Αφηγήτρια: Ιωάννα Β. Μεταξά, Πρόλογος: Guy (Michel) Saunier, Επιμέλεια: Τριαντάφυλλος Ε. Σκλαβενίτης, Εταιρεία Λευκαδικών Μελετών, Αθήνα.

Sourvinou-Inwood Ch., 1995, *"Reading" Greek Death. To the End of Classical Period*, Oxford.

Spiridakis G. Σπυριδάκης Γ., 1956, *Το τραγούδι των αιχμαλώτων του Τάταρη. Μοιρολόγι ή άσμα ιστορικόν*, Επετηρίς του Λαογραφικού Αρχείου, Τόμος 8 (1953–1954), 41–53.

Stathis E. Στάθης Ε., 2004, *Ελληνικά δημοτικά τραγούδια. Από τον ομηρικό μύθο και τ' αρχέτυπα σχήματα στους ρεμπέτες της Σμύρνης, της Θεσσαλονίκης και του Πειραιά*, Εκδόσεις Ι. Σιδέρης.

Stewart C., 1991, *Demons and the Devil: Moral Imagination in Modern Greek Culture*, Princeton.

Strimska M., 2005, *Modern Paganism in World Cultures: Comparative Perspectives (Religion in Contemporary Cultures)*, Santa Barbara, California.

Szyjewski A., 2003, *Religia Słowian*, Kraków.

Terpening R.H., 1985, *Charon and the Crossing. Ancient, Medieval and Renaissance Transformations of a Myth*, London–Toronto.

Tromp N.J., 1969, *Primitive Conceptions of Death and the Nether World in the Old Tetament*, Rome.

Tziovas D. (ed.), 2014, *Re-imagining the Past: Antiquity and Modern Greek Culture*, Oxford.

Van Tieghem Paul, 1948, *Le Romantisme - La Littérature Européenne*, Paris.

Vovelle M., 2008, *Śmierć w cywilizacji zachodu. Od roku 1300 po współczesność*, Gdańsk. [Originally published as: *La Mort et l'Occident de 1300 à nos jours*, Paris 1983.]

Vries A. de, 1974, *Dictionary of Symbols and Imagery*, North Holland.

Vryonis S., 1978, "Recent Scholarship on Continuity and Discontinuity of Culture: Classical Greeks, Byzantines, Modern Greeks," [in:] S. Vryonis (ed.), *The "Past" in Medieval and Modern Greek Culture*, Malibu, 237–256.

Waser O., 1898, *Charon, Charun, Charos*, Berlin.

Wrazas I., 2010, *Dyskomfort (nowo)Greków*, Wrocław.

Wrocławski K., 2011, "Narodowy i ponadnarodowy wymiar folkloru słowiańskiego," [in:] J. Rękas (ed.) *Bałkański folklor jako kod interkulturowy*, vol. 1, Poznań, 15–23.

Zadrożyńska A., Vražinovski T., 2002, *Ludowe obrzędy i podania. Etnograficzne i folklorystyczne studia porównawcze wsi polskiej i macedońskiej*, Warszawa.

APPENDIX

This appendix contains pictures taken in two cemeteries: in Corinth, in October 2009, and in Thessaloniki, in October 2016. The authentic writings, some of them as pieces of paper, laminated or just put into plastic document sleeves, and some engraved in stone, illustrate the vitality of sombre eschatological convictions as well as the presence of Charos in Modern Greek tradition.

Appendix 1.

With the breath you left
my little star, I will live.

And I will never see
again your smile.

As the sun I will enclose
both in my hands,
even if I break down,
I will speak of you!!!

As long as I live, I will love you
even in the earth
and if the dead
can feel, I will
love you still!!!

Your brother Stavros

Appendix 2.

About your unjust bereavement

On 29 March
of the year 1983
a little angel passed away
from the people.

It was a lively child
full of sweetness,
but you left so early
my little Mimika.

I had no right
to rejoice the world
and a wheel hit me
from the heavens.

My beloved parents,
I made you bitter with this
yet it was not my fault,
but I beg you.

Here, deep in the earth where I am lying,
when the evening comes
I am small and I can't,
I am afraid of darkness.

As I was afraid
when dusk was about to fall
and I ran to hide myself
in the arms of my mother.

That's why I beg you,
when the evening comes,
give me one minute
and light me a candle.

That's why, my sweet Mimika
I give you a promise
I will never let
your candle be extinguished.

My beloved parents
and you, good Giotoula
never forget that
I am your little sister.

With her I shared
bitterness and caresses
we played together tennis
in the neighbourhood in evenings.

But now, when you have lost her
you think a little of her
you bring to her grave
some flowers.

Ah, I wish you came one evening
ornamented as a bride
so that your mother could see you
because she is waiting.

She was not present, my Mimika
close to you at the funeral
it seems to her unbelievable
the whole story.

It was an unjust bereavement
it hurt us indeed
about such bereavements
we read in fables.

All your cousins
when they are together at home
they look at each other with sorrow
as if something is missing for them.

Their thoughts run once more,
Mimika, close to you,
yet the lips cannot
speak out your name.

Yet, whatever we will do,
you will not come back,
only in our thoughts
you will always be flying.

Ah, if I could one evening
come again to you

yet, I promise you,
I will come back in your dreams.
Those, who are forgotten, die.

Christos Tsantilas

Appendix 3.

Your traces, step by step,
are followed by your daughter and son.
Where are you going into this endless,
my father, night
and you leave us alone?
You seek a rosy bed
to sleep in the earth?
Where are you going, father, so handsome,
into this silence?
You think it is right
to make us orphans
in the warm and sweet embraces
of our mother?

Everything was ruined
the hopes and the dreams
a shape of you was left
a sweetness of your smile.
Joys in our souls have put out
[...] cemetery
[...] came in.

Your children

Appendix 4.

Fifty years you lived unclouded with him
you were the only love in his life
he adored you like a goddess, longed so that you didn't suffer
he boasted that he would not be able to live without you.

And you, like a turtle dove, who happened to lose her match,
and she cannot eat nor drink, only she wants to go to the woods,

looking for him all day long, waiting until he comes,
till in the end hungry and thirsty she dies.

Directly, as soon as Charos took your Takis (22.08.1970)
you did not endure even a year the burden of separation (17.04.1971)
You flew into Paradise to meet him (Holy Saturday)
wishing to give him a kiss of resurrection.

D.D.

* * *

Proofreading of the English text: Ian Corkill

Με τη ανάσα που αφησες
αστέρι μου θα ζω.

Και το χαμογελό σου
δεν θα το ξαναδώ.

Σαν ήλιο θα κλείσω
στα χέρια μου τα δυο
ακόμα κι αν λυγίσω
για σένα θα μιλώ!!!

Όσο θα ζω θα σ' αγαπώ
ακόμα και στο μνήμα
κι αν οι νεκροί
αισθάνονται θα
Σ' αγαπώ ακόμα!!!

Ο αδερφός σου Σταύρος

ΓΙΑ ΤΟΝ ΑΔΙΚΟ ΧΑΜΟ ΣΟΥ

Του Μάρτη στις 29
και του '83
ένα αγγελούδι έφυγε
από την κοινωνία.

Ήταν παιδάκι ζωηρό
γεμάτο [illegible] γλύκα
μα έφυγες πολύ νωρίς
μικρούλα μου Μιμίκα.

Δικαίωμα δεν είχα εγώ
τον κόσμο να χαρώ
κι ένας τροχός με κτύπησε
από τον ουρανό.

Αγαπημένοι μου γονείς
σας πίκρανα μ' αυτό
όμως εγώ δεν έφταιγα
μα σας παρακαλώ.

Εδώ βαθειά που κοίτομαι
σαν έρχεται το βράδυ
είμαι μικρό και δεν μπορώ
φοβάμαι το σκοτάδι.

Όπως και το φοβόμουνα
σαν έπεφτε η βραδυά
και στης μανούλας μου έτρεχα
να μπω στην αγκαλιά.

Για αυτό και σας παρακαλώ
σαι έρχεται το δείλι
χαρίστε μου ένα λεπτό
κι' ανάψτε το καιτήλι.

Γι' αυτό Μιμίκα μου γλυκειά
υπόσχεση σου δίνω
το καιτηλάκι σου σβηστώ
ποτέ να μην τ' αφήνω.

Αγαπημένοι μου γονείς
και εσύ καλέ Γιωτούλα
ποτέ σου να μην λησμονείς
είναι μια αδελφούλα.

Μαζί της μοιραζόσουνα
τις πίκρες και τα χάδια
μαζί ρακέτες έπαιζες
στην γειτονιά τα βράδυα.

Μα τώρα που την έχασες
την σκέπτεσαι λιγάκι
πηγαίνεις εις τον τάφο της
καιένα λουλουδάκι.

Αχ και ναρχόσουν μια βραδυά
νυφούλα στολισμένη
να σε έβλεπε η μανούλα σου
γιατί σε περιμένει.

Δεν ήτανε Μιμίκα μου
κοντά σου στην κηδεία
της φαίνεται απίστευτη
αυτή η ιστορία.

Ήτανε άδικος χαμός
μας πλήγωσε στ' αλήθεια
τέτοιους χαμούς διαβάζομε
μόνο στα παραμύθια.

Όλα τα ξαδερφάκια σου
σαν σμίγουνε στο σπίτι
κοιτάζονται περίλυπα
σαν κάτι να τους λείπει.

Τρέχει η σκέψη τους ξανά
Μιμίκα μου κοντά σου
όμως τα χείλη δεν μπορούν
να πούνε το όνομά σου.

Όμως ότι κι αν κάνομε
εσύ πια δεν γυρίζεις
μονάχα εις την σκέψη μας
πάντα θα φτερουγίζεις.

Αχ, να μπορούσα μια βραδυά
να ξαναρθώ κοντά σας
όμως σας το υπόσχομαι
θα 'ρθω στα όνειρά σας.

ΠΕΘΑΙΝΟΥΝ ΟΣΟΙ ΞΕΧΝΙΟΥΝΤΑΙ

ΧΡΗΣΤΟΣ ΤΣΑΝΤΗΛΑΣ

Τὰ ἴχνη σου βηματιστὰ
κόρη καὶ γυὸς ἀκολουθεῖ
Ποῦ πᾶς σ' αὐτὴ τὴν ἄπειρη
πατέρα μας νυχτιὰ
καὶ μόνους μᾶς ἀφηνεις;
Ζητᾶς κρεββάτι ρόδινο
νὰ κοιμηθῇς πάνω στὴ γῆ!
Ποῦ πᾶς πατέρα ἔτσι ὄμορφος
σ' αὐτὴ τὴ σιγαλιά;
Σωστὸ ἐσὺ τὸ κρίνεις
νὰ μᾶς ἀφήσῃς ὀρφανὰ
μὲς τῆς μαννούλας τὴ θερμὴ
κι' ὁλόγλυκη ἀγκαλιά;

ὅλα γκρεμίσθηκαν
οἱ ἐλπίδες τὰ ὄνειρα
ἡ μορφή σου ἀπόμεινε
τῶν χειλιῶν σου ἡ γλύκα.
Στ[illegible] ψυχή μας ἔσβυσαν οἱ χαρὲς
κ[illegible]όμερα
μ[illegible]ε κοιμητῆρι
λπ[illegible]ᾶς ἐμηκαν.

. τὰ παιδιά σου

ΠΕΝΗΝΤΑ ΧΡΟΝΙΑ ΕΖΗΣΕΣ ΑΝΕΦΕΛΑ ΜΑΖΙ ΤΟΥ
ΜΟΝΑΔΙΚΗ ΑΓΑΠΗ ΤΟΥ ΗΣΟΥΝΑ ΣΤΗ ΖΩΗ. ΤΟΥ
ΣΕ ΛΑΤΡΕΥΕ ΩΣΑΝ ΘΕΑ ΜΗΝ ΠΑΘΗΣ ΛΑΧΤΑΡΟΥΣΕ
ΧΩΡΙΣ ΕΣΕ ΚΑΥΧΙΩΤΑΝΕ ΝΑ ΖΗΣΗ ΔΕΝ ΜΠΟΡΟΥΣΕ

ΣΥ ΣΑΝ ΤΡΥΓΩΝΑ ΠΟΥ ΑΝ ΣΥΜΒΗ ΤΟ ΤΑΙΡΙ ΤΗΣ ΝΑ ΧΑΣΗ
ΟΥΔΕ ΝΑ ΦΑΗ ΟΥΔΕ ΝΑ ΠΙΗ ΘΕΛΕΙ ΜΟΝ ΜΕΣ' ΤΑ ΔΑΣΗ
ΟΛΗΜΕΡΙΣ ΤΟ ΑΝΑΖΗΤΑ ΚΑΙ ΝΑΡΘΗ ΤΟ ΠΡΟΣΜΕΝΕΙ
ΜΕΧΡΙΣ ΠΟΥ ΤΕΛΟΣ ΝΗΣΤΙΚΗ ΚΙ ΑΠΟΤΙΣΤΗ ΠΕΘΑΙΝΕΙ

ΕΥΘΥΣ ΜΟΛΙΣ ΤΟΝ ΤΑΚΗ ΣΟΥ ΣΩΥ ΤΟΝ ΕΠΗΡΕ Ο ΧΑΡΟΣ (22·8·70)
ΟΥΤΕ ΕΝΑΝ ΧΡΟΝΟ ΒΑΣΤΑΞΕΣ ΤΟΥ ΧΩΡΙΣΜΟΥ ΤΟ ΒΑΡΟΣ (17·4·71)
ΠΕΤΑΞΕΣ ΣΤΟΝ ΠΑΡΑΔΕΙΣΟ ΓΙΑ ΝΑ ΤΟΝ ΑΝΤΑΜΩΣΗΣ (Μ. ΣΑΒΒΑΤΟ)
ΦΙΛΙ ΤΗΣ ΑΝΑΣΤΑΣΕΩΣ ΘΕΛΟΝΤΑΣ ΝΑ ΤΟΥ ΔΩΣΗΣ

Δ. Δ.

COPY EDITOR
Karolina Wąsowska

PROOFREADER
Małgorzata Szul

TYPOGRAPHIC DESIGN
Wojciech Wojewoda

Jagiellonian University Press
Editorial Offices: Michałowskiego 9/2, 31-126 Kraków
Phone: +48 12 663 23 80, +48 12 663 23 82, Fax: +48 12 663 23 83